JOHN DO

Selections from his poetry and prose

JOHN DONNE

Selections from his poetry and prose

Edited by Robert Van de Weyer

Fount
An Imprint of HarperCollins*Publishers*

Fount Paperbacks is an Imprint of
HarperCollins*Religious*
Part of HarperCollins*Publishers*
77–85 Fulham Palace Road, London W6 8JB

First published in Great Britain
in 1995 by Fount Paperbacks

1 3 5 7 9 10 8 6 4 2

A catalogue record for this book is
available from the British Library

ISBN 0 00 627923-6

Printed and bound in Great Britain by
HarperCollinsManufacturing Glasgow

Contents

Introduction

John Donne was famous in his day as a rascal, a witty pamphleteer, and, in his later years, a preacher of great learning and spiritual insight. His poetry, written not for publication, but to unburden himself of his intense emotions, was for the most part known only to close friends. His reputation sank in the decades after his death, and for over two and a half centuries he was largely forgotten. But in the early years of this century young poets, such as W. B. Yeats and T. S. Eliot, rediscovered Donne's verse, finding in it a blend of passion and intellectual vigour which they sought to emulate. Thus, through the voice of modern poetry, Donne has at last gained the place he deserves, amongst the first rank of English writers.

Donne was born some time in the first half of 1572. His parents were both Roman Catholics; his mother was related to Sir Thomas More, two of his uncles were Jesuits who died in exile, and his younger brother was imprisoned for sheltering a Catholic priest. But despite such powerful family influences, the young John Donne believed himself to be indifferent to religion; and he dropped Catholicism to become a member of the Church of England, in order to advance his career as a lawyer and a diplomat. In 1592 he became a law student at Lincoln's Inn, attracting attention by his quick wit and dissolute habits: as a senior member of the Inn described him, he was 'a great visitor of ladies, a great frequenter of plays, and a great writer of comic verses'. He joined the Earl of Essex and Sir Walter Raleigh on a sea expedition in 1596-7 during the prolonged war against Spain, writing journalistic reports which were widely read in England. On his return he entered the service of Sir Thomas Egerton, soon to become Lord

Chancellor; and he now seemed destined for a glittering career.

But his passion undermined his ambition. In December 1601 he secretly married Ann More, the young niece of his employer's wife. Sir Thomas immediately dismissed him; and Ann's father had Donne imprisoned for marrying a minor without parental consent. On his release Donne was penniless, and thirteen years of wretched poverty followed. He and Ann lived in a damp cottage south of London, and Ann bore him twelve children. He earned a meagre living by his pen, writing articles and tracts against Catholic doctrine at the behest of Protestant patrons. In the process he became one of the most learned theologians of his day, and one of his anti-Catholic pieces even won him an honorary degree at Oxford. But to Donne himself theological controversy was little more than an intellectual game.

The lasting fruit of this period is, however, his *Songs and Sonnets.* The dominant theme of these poems is the love of a man for a woman; and one assumes his devotion to Ann is the inspiration. Yet even in his most passionate and erotic verses, metaphysical and moral questions constantly emerge. At times he tries to suppress these concerns with wit and erudition, and seems simply to be playing with words. But taken as a whole the poems tell the story of a soul still immersed in worldly ambitions and desires, and at the same time reaching upwards towards a higher plane of intellect and emotion. And the dramatic images and phrases, combined with the artistry of metre and rhyme, give the poems astonishing power.

To our knowledge there was no religious crisis in Donne's life, no moment of conversion. He himself saw his marriage as the turning-point. In his devotion to Ann, bodily desire and spiritual love were unified: the unity of body and spirit is the constant theme of his love poetry. And gradually he came to perceive God as the source of this unity. As early as 1610 his friends were urging him to seek ordination, and he still had ambitions for a secular career. But in his poetry religious themes begin to dominate, and his *Divine Poems* belong to this period. 'La Corona' is a linked sequence on the mysteries of the Christian faith. And in the 'Holy Sonnets' his passion, wit and poetic skill are directed to the traditional subjects of meditation: sin, death and judgement.

King James himself, impressed by Donne's theological essays, finally persuaded Donne to take holy orders in 1615. His faith was deepened by Ann's death at the age of thirty-three. In his grief he saw himself as being crucified for his sins; and he came to regard his past life as God's wooing of him, his sufferings and setbacks being God's 'corrections' in which he 'burns off the rust of my deformity'. Finally his grief turned into 'joy and rest in the peace of Christ'. After Ann's death he wrote little poetry, and his creative impulse was directed towards preaching. In 1621 he was appointed Dean of St Paul's Cathedral in London. And in the following decade he gained the reputation of being the finest preacher in the land; the new king, Charles I, chose Donne to preach the first sermon of his reign. The dense language, the strong repetitive rhythms, and the striking images of his sermons are reminiscent of his poetry: and, like his poems, his sermons are filled with psychological insights. Yet all these qualities are within the framework of theological argument, in which references to the scriptures and to the early fathers are used to elucidate Christian doctrine.

Some of his sermons were published during his lifetime, and enjoyed wide circulation. Also in 1624 his *Devotions on Emergent Occasions* appeared, the fruit of a serious illness the previous winter. Each Devotion begins with a meditation in which Donne reflects on his sickness and his emotions towards it; there follows an Expostulation in which he debates his situation with God; and his thoughts and feelings are finally resolved in a Prayer. To the modern reader his devotions are more accessible than his sermons; and phrases from them have passed into our common parlance.

Donne preached his final sermon in February 1631, a month before his death. It was published posthumously under the title 'Death's Duel'. He was visibly dying, and it was remarked afterwards that 'Dr Donne hath preached his own funeral sermon'. Shortly before he died he wrote his own epitaph, and had his portrait painted in his death shroud. In the following year the picture was used to make a statue of him, to stand in the cathedral. When in the Great Fire of 1666 the cathedral was burnt down, Donne's statue was the only monument to survive. His epitaph, carved below, describes his 'looking towards Him whose name is the Rising'.

Songs and Sonnets

John Donne - did not want to be known as prof. writer. Around time of Shakespeare. Not part of court but in grp who are around court trying to impress.

Doesn't use flattery/pity - instead arguements. Make you see arguement progressing in person's mind. Uses it as a tool of seduction. Persuasion

AIR AND ANGELS

Twice or thrice had I loved thee,
Before I knew thy face or name;
So in a voice, so in a shapeless flame,
Angels affect us oft, and worshipped be;
  Still when, to where thou wert, I came,
Some lovely glorious nothing I did see,
  But since my soul, whose child love is,
Takes limbs of flesh, and else could nothing do,
  More subtle than the parent is
Love must not be, but take a body too,
  And therefore what thou wert, and who
    I bid love ask, and now
That it assume thy body, I allow,
And fix itself in thy lip, eye, and brow.

Whilst thus to ballast love, I thought,
And so more steadily to have gone,
With wares which would sink admiration,
I saw, I had love's pinnace overfraught,
  Every thy hair for love to work upon
Is much too much, some fitter must be sought;
  For, nor in nothing, nor in things
Extreme, as scatt'ring bright, can love inhere;
  Then as an angel, face and wings
Of air, not pure as it, yet pure doth wear,
  So thy love may be my love's sphere;
    Just such disparity
As is 'twixt air and angels' purity,
'Twixt women's love, and men's will ever be.

THE ANNIVERSARY

All kings, and all their favourites,
All glory of honours, beauties, wits,
The sun itself, which makes times, as they pass,
Is elder by a year, now, than it was
When thou and I first one another saw:
All other things, to their destruction draw,
Only our love hath no decay;
This, no tomorrow hath, nor yesterday,
Running it never runs from us away,
But truly keeps his first, last, everlasting day.

Two graves must hide thine and my corse,
If one might, death were no divorce,
Alas, as well as other princes, we,
(Who prince enough in one another be,)
Must leave at last in death, these eyes, and ears,
Oft fed with true oaths, and with sweet salt tears;
But souls where nothing dwells but love
(All other thoughts being inmates) then shall prove
This, or a love increased there above,
When bodies to their graves, souls from their graves
remove.

And then we shall be throughly blessed,
But we no more, than all the rest,
Here upon earth, we are kings, and none but we
Can be such kings, nor of such subjects be;
Who is so safe as we? where none can do
Treason to us, except one of us two.
True and false fears let us refrain,
Let us love nobly, and live, and add again
Years and years unto years, till we attain
To write threescore, this is the second of our reign.

THE APPARITION

When by thy scorn, O murderess, I am dead,
And that thou think'st thee free
From all solicitation from me,
Then shall my ghost come to thy bed,
And thee, feigned vestal, in worse arms shall see;
Then thy sick taper will begin to wink,
And he, whose thou art then, being tired before,
Will, if thou stir, or pinch to wake him, think
  Thou call'st for more,
And in false sleep will from thee shrink,
And then poor aspen wretch, neglected thou
Bathed in a cold quicksilver sweat wilt lie
  A verier ghost than I;
What I will say, I will not tell thee now,
Lest that preserve thee; and since my love is spent,
I had rather thou shouldst painfully repent,
Than by my threatenings rest still innocent.

THE CANONIZATION

For God's sake hold your tongue, and let me love,
Or chide my palsy, or my gout,
My five grey hairs, or ruined fortune flout,
With wealth your state, your mind with arts
improve,
Take you a course, get you a place,
Observe his Honour, or his Grace,
Or the King's real, or his stampèd face
Contemplate; what you will, approve,
So you will let me love.

Alas, alas, who's injured by my love?
What merchant's ships have my sighs drowned?
Who says my tears have overflowed his ground?
When did my colds a forward spring remove?
When did the heats which my veins fill
Add one more to the plaguy bill?
Soldiers find wars, and lawyers find out still
Litigious men, which quarrels move,
Though she and I do love.

Call us what you will, we are made such by love;
Call her one, me another fly,
We are tapers too, and at our own cost die,
And we in us find the eagle and the dove,
The phoenix riddle hath more wit
By us; we two being one, are it.
So to one neutral thing both sexes fit
We die and rise the same, and prove
Mysterious by this love.

We can die by it, if not live by love,
  And if unfit for tombs and hearse
Our legend be, it will be fit for verse;
And if no piece of chronicle we prove,
  We'll build in sonnets pretty rooms;
  As well a well wrought urn becomes
The greatest ashes, as half-acre tombs,
  And by these hymns, all shall approve
  Us canonized for love:

And thus invoke us; 'You whom reverend love
  Made one another's hermitage;
You, to whom love was peace, that now is rage;
  Who did the whole world's soul contract, and
    drove
    Into the glasses of your eyes
    (So made such mirrors, and such spies,
That they did all to you epitomize,)
  Countries, towns, courts: beg from above
  A pattern of your love!'

COMMUNITY

Good we must love, and must hate ill,
For ill is ill, and good good still,
But there are things indifferent,
Which we may neither hate, nor love,
But one, and then another prove,
As we shall find our fancy bent.

If then at first wise Nature had
Made women either good or bad,
Then some we might hate, and some choose,
But since she did them so create,
That we may neither love, nor hate,
Only this rests, All, all may use.

If they were good it would be seen,
Good is as visible as green,
And to all eyes itself betrays:
If they were bad, they could not last,
Bad doth itself, and others waste,
So, they deserve nor blame, nor praise.

But they are ours as fruits are ours,
He that but tastes, he that devours,
And he that leaves all, doth as well:
Changed loves are but changed sorts of meat,
And when he hath the kernel eat,
Who doth not fling away the shell?

THE DAMP

When I am dead, and doctors know not why,
And my friends' curiosity
Will have me cut up to survey each part,
When they shall find your picture in my heart,
You think a sudden damp of love
Will through all their senses move,
And work on them as me, and so prefer
Your murder, to the name of massacre.

Poor victories; but if you dare be brave,
And pleasure in your conquest have,
First kill th' enormous giant, your Disdain,
And let th' enchantress Honour, next be slain,
And like a Goth and Vandal rise,
Deface records, and histories
Of your own arts and triumphs over men,
And without such advantage kill me then.

For I could muster up as well as you
My giants, and my witches too,
Which are vast Constancy, and Secretness,
But these I neither look for, nor profess;
Kill me as woman, let me die
As a mere man; do you but try
Your passive valour, and you shall find then,
Naked you have odds enough of any man.

THE DREAM

Dear love, for nothing less than thee
Would I have broke this happy dream,
  It was a theme
For reason, much too strong for phantasy,
Therefore thou waked'st me wisely; yet
My dream thou brok'st not, but continued'st it:
Thou art so true, that thoughts of thee suffice,
To make dreams truths, and fables histories;
Enter these arms, for since thou thought'st it best,
Not to dream all my dream, let's act the rest.

As lightning, or a taper's light,
Thine eyes, and not thy noise waked me;
  Yet I thought thee
(For thou lov'st truth) an angel, at first sight,
But when I saw thou saw'st my heart,
And knew'st my thoughts, beyond an angel's art,
When thou knew'st what I dreamed, when thou
  knew'st when
Excess of joy would wake me, and cam'st then,
I must confess, it could not choose but be
Profane, to think thee anything but thee.

Coming and staying showed thee, thee,
But rising makes me doubt, that now,
  Thou art not thou.
That love is weak, where fear's as strong as he;
'Tis not all spirit, pure, and brave,
If mixture it of fear, shame, honour, have.
Perchance as torches which must ready be,
Men light and put out, so thou deal'st with me,
Thou cam'st to kindle, goest to come; then I
Will dream that hope again, but else would die.

THE ECSTASY

Where, like a pillow on a bed,
  A pregnant bank swelled up, to rest
The violet's reclining head,
  Sat we two, one another's best;

Our hands were firmly cemented
  With a fast balm, which thence did spring,
Our eye-beams twisted, and did thread
  Our eyes, upon one double string;

So to' intergraft our hands, as yet
  Was all our means to make us one,
And pictures in our eyes to get
  Was all our propagation.

As 'twixt two equal armies, Fate
  Suspends uncertain victory,
Our souls, (which to advance their state,
  Were gone out), hung 'twixt her, and me.

And whilst our souls negotiate there,
  We like sepulchral statues lay;
All day, the same our postures were,
  And we said nothing, all the day.

If any, so by love refined,
  That he soul's language understood,
And by good love were grown all mind,
  Within convenient distance stood,

He (though he knew not which soul spake
  Because both meant, both spake the same)
Might thence a new concoction take,
  And part far purer than he came.

This ecstasy doth unperplex
  (We said) and tell us what we love,
We see by this, it was not sex,
  We see, we saw not what did move:

But as all several souls contain
  Mixture of things, they know not what,
Love, these mixed souls doth mix again,
  And makes both one, each this and that.

A single violet transplant,
  The strength, the colour, and the size,
(All which before was poor, and scant,)
  Redoubles still, and multiplies.

When love, with one another so
  Interinanimates two souls,
That abler soul, which thence doth flow,
  Defects of loneliness controls.

We then, who are this new soul, know,
  Of what we are composed, and made,
For, th' atomies of which we grow,
  Are souls, whom no change can invade.

But O alas, so long, so far
  Our bodies why do we forbear?
They are ours, though they are not we, we are
  The intelligences, they the sphere.

We owe them thanks, because they thus,
  Did us, to us, at first convey,
Yielded their forces, sense, to us,
  Nor are dross to us, but allay.

On man heaven's influence works not so,
  But that it first imprints the air,
So soul into the soul may flow,
  Though it to body first repair.

As our blood labours to beget
  Spirits, as like souls as it can,
Because such fingers need to knit
  That subtle knot, which makes us man:

So must pure lovers' souls descend
  T' affections, and to faculties,
Which sense may reach and apprehend,
  Else a great prince in prison lies.

To our bodies turn we then, that so
  Weak men on love revealed may look;
Love's mysteries in souls do grow,
  But yet the body is his book.

And if some lover, such as we,
  Have heard this dialogue of one,
Let him still mark us, he shall see
  Small change, when we'are to bodies gone.

THE EXPIRATION

So, so, break off this lamenting kiss,
Which sucks two souls, and vapours both away,
Turn thou ghost that way, and let me turn this,
And let ourselves benight our happiest day,
We asked none leave to love; nor will we owe
Any, so cheap a death, as saying, Go;

Go; and if that word have not quite killed thee,
Ease me with death, by bidding me go too.
Oh, if it have, let my word work on me,
And a just office on a murderer do.
Except it be too late, to kill me so,
Being double dead, going, and bidding, go.

FAREWELL TO LOVE

Whilst yet to prove,
I thought there was some deity in love
So did I reverence, and gave
Worship; as atheists at their dying hour
Call, what they cannot name, an unknown power,
As ignorantly did I crave:
Thus when
Things not yet known are coveted by men,
Our desires give them fashion, and so
As they wax lesser, fall, as they size, grow.

But, from late fair
His highness sitting in a golden chair,
Is not less cared for after three days
By children, than the thing which lovers so
Blindly admire,and with such worship woo;
Being had, enjoying it decays:
And thence,
What before pleased them all, takes but one sense,
And that so lamely, as it leaves behind
A kind of sorrowing dullness to the mind.

Ah cannot we,
As well as cocks and lions jocund be,
After such pleasures? Unless wise
Nature decreed (since each such act, they say,
Diminisheth the length of life a day)
This; as she would man should despise
The sport,
Because that other curse of being short,
And only for a minute made to be
Eager, desires to raise posterity.

Since so, my mind
Shall not desire what no man else can find,
I'll no more dote and run
To pursue things which had endamaged me.
And when I come where moving beauties be,
As men do when the summer's sun
Grows great,
Though I admire their greatness, shun their heat;
Each place can afford shadows. If all fail,
'Tis but applying worm-seed to the tail.

A FEVER

Oh do not die, for I shall hate
  All women so, when thou art gone,
That thee I shall not celebrate,
  When I remember, thou wast one.

But yet thou canst not die, I know,
  To leave this world behind, is death,
But when thou from this world wilt go,
  The whole world vapours with thy breath.

Or if, when thou, the world's soul, go'st,
  It stay, 'tis but thy carcase then,
The fairest woman, but thy ghost,
  But corrupt worms, the worthiest men.

Oh wrangling schools, that search what fire
  Shall burn this world, had none the wit
Unto this knowledge to aspire,
  That this her fever might be it?

And yet she cannot waste by this,
  Nor long bear this torturing wrong,
For much corruption needful is
  To fuel such a fever long.

These burning fits but meteors be,
  Whose matter in thee is soon spent.
Thy beauty, and all parts, which are thee,
  Are changeable firmament.

Yet 'twas of my mind, seizing thee,
  Though it in thee cannot persèver.
For I had rather owner be
  Of thee one hour, than all else ever.

JOHN DONNE

THE FLEA

Mark but this flea, and mark in this,
How little that which thou deny'st me is;
Me it sucked first, and now sucks thee,
And in this flea, our two bloods mingled be;
Confess it, this cannot be said
A sin, or shame, or loss of maidenhead,
  Yet this enjoys before it woo,
  And pampered swells with one blood made of two,
And this, alas, is more than we would do.

Oh stay, three lives in one flea spare,
Where we almost, nay more than married are.
This flea is you and I, and this
Our marriage bed, and marriage temple is;
Though parents grudge, and you, we'are met,
And cloistered in these living walls of jet.
  Though use make you apt to kill me,
  Let not to this, self murder added be,
  And sacrilege, three sins in killing three.

Cruel and sudden, hast thou since
Purpled thy nail, in blood of innocence?
In what could this flea guilty be,
Except in that drop, which it sucked from thee?
Yet thou triumph'st, and say'st that thou
Find'st not thyself, nor me the weaker now;
  'Tis true, then learn how false, fears be;
  Just so much honour, when thou yield'st to me,
  Will waste, as this flea's death took life from thee.

THE FUNERAL

Whoever comes to shroud me, do not harm
Nor question much
That subtle wreath of hair, which crowns my arm;
The mystery, the sign you must not touch,
For 'tis my outward soul,
Viceroy to that, which then to heaven being gone,
Will leave this to control,
And keep these limbs, her provinces, from dissolution.

For if the sinewy thread my brain lets fall
Through every part,
Can tie those parts, and make me one of all;
These hairs which upward grew, and strength and art
Have from a better brain,
Can better do it; except she meant that I
By this should know my pain,
As prisoners then are manacled, when they are
condemned to die.

Whate'er she meant by it, bury it with me,
For since I am
Love's martyr, it might breed idolatry,
If into others' hands these relics came;
As 'twas humility
To afford to it all that a soul can do,
So, 'tis some bravery,
That since you would save none of me, I bury some
of you.

THE GOOD MORROW

I wonder by my troth, what thou, and I
  Did, till we loved? were we not weaned till then,
But sucked on country pleasures, childishly?
  Or snorted we in the seven sleepers' den?
'Twas so; but this, all pleasures fancies be.
If ever any beauty I did see,
Which I desired, and got, 'twas but a dream of thee.

And now good morrow to our waking souls,
  Which watch not one another out of fear;
For love, all love of other sights controls,
  And makes one little room, an every where.
Let sea-discoverers to new worlds have gone,
Let maps to others, worlds on worlds have shown,
Let us possess one world, each hath one, and is one.

My face in thine eye, thine in mine appears,
  And true plain hearts do in the faces rest,
Where can we find two better hemispheres
  Without sharp north, without declining west?
What ever dies, was not mixed equally;
If our two loves be one, or, thou and I
Love so alike, that none do slacken, none can die.

A JET RING SENT

Thou art not so black, as my heart,
Nor half so brittle, as her heart, thou art;
What wouldst thou say? Shall both our properties by
thee be spoke,
Nothing more endless, nothing sooner broke?

Marriage rings are not of this stuff;
Oh, why should aught less precious, or less tough
Figure our loves? Except in thy name thou have bid it say,
I am cheap, and naught but fashion, fling me away.

Yet stay with me since thou art come,
Circle this finger's top, which didst her thumb.
Be justly proud, and gladly safe, that thou dost dwell
with me,
She that, oh, broke her faith, would soon break thee.

LOVERS' INFINITENESS

If yet I have not all thy love,
Dear, I shall never have it all,
I cannot breathe one other sigh, to move,
Nor can entreat one other tear to fall.
All my treasure, which should purchase thee,
Sighs, tears, and oaths, and letters I have spent,
Yet no more can be due to me,
Than at the bargain made was meant.
If then thy gift of love were partial,
That some to me, some should to others fall,
   Dear, I shall never have thee all.

Or if then thou gavest me all,
All was but all, which thou hadst then;
But if in thy heart, since, there be or shall
New love created be, by other men,
Which have their stocks entire, and can in tears,
In sighs, in oaths, and letters outbid me,
This new love may beget new fears,
For, this love was not vowed by thee.
And yet it was, thy gift being general,
The ground, thy heart is mine; whatever shall
   Grow there, dear, I should have it all.

Yet I would not have all yet,
He that hath all can have no more,
And since my love doth every day admit
New growth, thou shouldst have new rewards in store;
Thou canst not every day give me thy heart,
If thou canst give it, then thou never gav'st it:
Love's riddles are, that though thy heart depart,
It stays at home, and thou with losing sav'st it:
But we will have a way more liberal,
Than changing hearts, to join them, so we shall
   Be one, and one another's all.

LOVE'S ALCHEMY

Some that have deeper digged love's mine than I,
Say, where his centric happiness doth lie:
I have loved, and got, and told,
But should I love, get, tell, till I were old,
I should not find that hidden mystery;
Oh, 'tis imposture all:
And as no chemic yet the elixir got,
But glorifies his pregnant pot,
If by the way to him befall
Some odoriferous thing, or medicinal,
So, lovers dream a rich and long delight,
But get a winter-seeming summer's night.

Our ease, our thrift, our honour, and our day,
Shall we, for this vain bubble's shadow pay?
Ends love in this, that my man,
Can be as happy as I can; if he can
Endure the short scorn of a bridegroom's play?
That loving wretch that swears,
'Tis not the bodies marry, but the minds,
Which he in her angelic finds,
Would swear as justly, that he hears,
In that day's rude hoarse ministrelsy, the spheres.
Hope not for mind in women; at their best
Sweetness and wit, they are but mummy, possessed.

LOVE'S GROWTH

I scarce believe my love to be so pure
  As I had thought it was,
  Because it doth endure
Vicissitude, and season, as the grass;
Methinks I lied all winter, when I swore,
My love was infinite, if spring make it more.
But if this medicine, love, which cures all sorrow
With more, not only be no quintessence,
But mixed of all stuffs, paining soul, or sense,
And of the sun his working vigour borrow,
Love's not so pure, and abstract, as they use
To say, which have no mistress but their Muse,
But as all else, being elemented too,
Love sometimes would contemplate, sometimes do.

And yet not greater, but more eminent,
  Love by the spring is grown;
  As, in the firmament,
Stars by the sun are not enlarged, but shown,
Gentle love deeds, as blossoms on a bough,
From love's awakened root do bud out now.
If, as in water stirred more circles be
Produced by one, love such additions take,
Those like so many spheres, but one heaven make,
For, they are all concentric unto thee,
And though each spring do add to love new heat,
As princes do in times of action get
New taxes, and remit them not in peace,
No winter shall abate the spring's increase.

A NOCTURNAL UPON ST LUCY'S DAY, BEING THE SHORTEST DAY

'Tis the year's midnight, and it is the day's
Lucy's, who scarce seven hours herself unmasks,
The sun is spent, and now his flasks
Send forth light squibs, no contrast rays;
The world's whole sap is sunk:
The general balm th' hydroptic earth hath drunk,
Whither, as to the bed's-feet, life is shrunk,
Dead and interred; yet all these seem to laugh,
Compared with me, who am their epitaph.

Study me then, you who shall lovers be
At the next world, that is, at the next spring:
For I am every dead thing,
In whom love wrought new alchemy.
For his art did express
A quintessence even from nothingness,
From dull privations, and lean emptiness
He ruined me, and I am re-begot
Of absence, darkness, death; things which are not.

All others, from all things, draw all that's good,
Life, soul, form, spirit, whence they being have;
I, by love's limbeck, am the grave
Of all, that's nothing. Oft a flood
Have we two wept, and so
Drowned the whole world, us two; oft did we grow
To be two chaoses, when we did show
Care to aught else; and often absences
Withdrew our souls, and made us carcases.

But I am by her death (which word wrongs her)
Of the first nothing, the elixir grown;
  Were I a man, that I were one,
  I needs must know; I should prefer,
    If I were any beast,
Some ends, some means; yea plants, yea stones
  detest,
And love; all, all some properties invest;
If I an ordinary nothing were,
As shadow, a light, and body must be here.

But I am none; nor will my sun renew.
You lovers, for whose sake, the lesser sun
  At this time to the Goat is run
  To fetch new lust, and give it you,
    Enjoy your summer all;
Since she enjoys her long night's festival,
Let me prepare towards her, and let me call
This hour her vigil, and her eve, since this
Both the year's, and the day's deep midnight is.

THE PARADOX

No lover saith, I love, nor any other
  Can judge a perfect lover;
He thinks that else none can, nor will agree
  That any loves but he:
I cannot say I loved, for who can say
  He was killed yesterday?
Love with excess of heat, more young than old,
  Death kills with too much cold;
We die but once, and who loved last did die,
  He that saith twice, doth lie:
For though he seem to move, and stir a while,
  It doth the sense beguile.
Such life is like the light which bideth yet
  When the light's life is set,
Or like the heat, which fire in solid matter
  Leaves behind, two hours after.
Once I loved and died; and am now become
  Mine epitaph and tomb.
Here dead men speak their last, and so do I;
  Love-slain, lo, here I lie.

THE RELIC

When my grave is broke up again
Some second guest to entertain,
(For graves have learned that woman-head
To be to more than one a bed)
And he that digs it, spies
A bracelet of bright hair about the bone,
Will he not let us alone,
And think that there a loving couple lies,
Who thought that this device might be some way
To make their souls, at the last busy day,
Meet at this grave, and make a little stay?
If this fall in a time, or land,
Where mis-devotion doth command,
Then, he that digs us up, will bring
Us, to the Bishop, and the King,
To make us relics; then
Thou shalt be a Mary Magdalen, and I
A something else thereby;
All women shall adore us, and some men;
And since at such time, miracles are sought,
I would have that age by this paper taught
What miracles we harmless lovers wrought.

First, we loved well and faithfully,
Yet knew not what we loved, nor why,
Difference of sex no more we knew,
Than our guardian angels do;
Coming and going, we
Perchance might kiss, but not between those meals;
Our hands ne'er touched the seals,
Which nature, injured by late law, sets free:
These miracles we did; but now alas,
All measure, and all language, I should pass,
Should I tell what a miracle she was.

SONG

Go, and catch a falling star,
Get with child a mandrake root,
Tell me, where all past years are,
Or who cleft the Devil's foot,
Teach me to hear mermaids singing,
Or to keep off envy's stinging,
And find
What wind
Serves to advance an honest mind.

If thou be'est born to strange sights,
Things invisible to see,
Ride ten thousand days and nights,
Till age snow white hairs on thee,
Thou, when thou return'st, wilt tell me
All strange wonders that befall thee,
And swear
No where
Lives a woman true, and fair.

If thou find'st one, let me know,
Such a pilgrimage were sweet,
Yet do not, I would not go,
Though at next door we might meet,
Though she were true, when you met her,
And last, till you write your letter,
Yet she
Will be
False, ere I come, to two, or three.

SONG

Sweetest love, I do not go,
For weariness of thee,
Nor in hope the world can show
A fitter love for me;
But since that I
Must die at last, 'tis best,
To use my self in jest
Thus by feigned deaths to die.

Yesternight the sun went hence,
And yet is here today,
He hath no desire nor sense,
Nor half so short a way:
Then fear not me,
But believe that I shall make
Speedier journeys, since I take
More wings and spurs than he.

O how feeble is man's power,
That if good fortune fall,
Cannot add another hour,
Nor a lost hour recall!
But come bad chance,
And we join to it our strength,
And we teach it art and length,
Itself o'er us to advance.

When thou sigh'st, thou sigh'st not wind,
But sigh'st my soul away,
When thou weep'st, unkindly kind,
My life's blood doth decay.
It cannot be
That thou lov'st me, as thou say'st,
If in thine my life thou waste,

Thou art the best of me.
Let not thy divining heart
Forethink me any ill,
Destiny may take thy part,
And may thy fears fulfil;
But think that we
Are but turned aside to sleep;
They who one another keep
Alive, ne'er parted be.

THE SUN RISING

Busy old fool, unruly sun,
Why dost thou thus,
Through windows, and through curtains call on us?
Must to thy motions lovers' seasons run?
Saucy pedantic wretch, go chide
Late school-boys, and sour prentices,
Go tell court-huntsmen, that the King will ride,
Call country ants to harvest offices;
Love, all alike, no season knows, nor clime,
Nor hours, days, months, which are the rags of time.

Thy beams, so reverend, and strong
Why shouldst thou think?
I could eclipse and cloud them with a wink,
But that I would not lose her sight so long:
If her eyes have not blinked thine,
Look, and tomorrow late, tell me,
Whether both th'Indias of spice and mine
Be where thou left'st them, or lie here with me.
Ask for those kinds whom thou saw'st yesterday,
And thou shalt hear, All here in one bed lay.

She'is all states, and all princes, I,
Nothing else is.
Princes do but play us; compared to this,
All honour's mimic; all wealth alchemy.
Thou sun art half as happy as we,
In that the world's contracted thus;
Thine age asks ease, and since thy duties be
To warm the world, that's done in warming us.
Shine here to us, and thou art everywhere;
This bed thy centre is, these walls, thy sphere.

THE TRIPLE FOOL

I am two fools, I know,
For loving, and for saying so
In whining poetry;
But where's that wiseman, that would not be I,
If she would not deny?
Then as th'earth's inward narrow crooked lanes
Do purge sea water's fretful salt away,
I thought, if I could draw my pains
Through rhyme's vexation, I should them allay.
Grief brought to numbers cannot be so fierce,
For, he tames it, that fetters it in verse.

But when I have done so,
Some man, his art and voice to show,
Doth set and sing my pain,
And, by delighting many, frees again
Grief, which verse did restrain.
To love and grief tribute of verse belongs,
But not of such as pleases when 'tis read,
Both are increased by such songs:
For both their triumphs so are published,
And I, which was two fools, do so grow three;
Who are a little wise, the best fools be.

JOHN DONNE

TWICKNAM GARDEN

Blasted with sighs, and surrounded with tears,
Higher I come to seek the spring,
And at mine eyes, and at mine ears,
Receive such balms, as else cure everything;
But O, self traitor, I do bring
The spider love, which transubstantiates all,
And can convert manna to gall,
And that this place may thoroughly be thought
True paradise, I have the serpent brought.

'Twere wholesomer for me, that winter did
Benight the glory of this place,
And that a grave frost did forbid
These trees to laugh, and mock me to my face;
But that I may not this disgrace
Endure, nor yet leave loving, Love, let me
Some senseless piece of this place be;
Make me a mandrake, so I may groan here,
Or a stone fountain weeping out my year.

Hither with crystal vials, lovers come,
And take my tears, which are love's wine,
And try your mistress' tears at home,
For all are false, that taste not just like mine;
Alas, hearts do not in eyes shine,
Nor can you more judge woman's thoughts by tears,
Than by her shadow, what she wears.
O perverse sex, where none is true but she,
Who's therefore true, because her truth kills me.

THE UNDERTAKING

I have done one braver thing
Than all the Worthies did,
And yet a braver thence doth spring,
Which is, to keep that hid.

It were but madness now t'impart
The skill of specular stone,
When he which can have learned the art
To cut it, can find none.

So, if I now should utter this,
Others (because no more
Such stuff to work upon, there is,)
Would love but as before.

But he who loveliness within
Hath found, all outward loathes,
For he who colour loves, and skin,
Loves but their oldest clothes.

If, as I have, you also do
Virtue attired in woman see,
And dare love that, and say so too,
And forget the He and She;

And if this love, though placed so,
From profane men you hide,
Which will no faith on this bestow,
Or, if they do, deride:

Then you have done a braver thing
Than all the Worthies did,
And a braver thence will spring,
Which is, to keep that hid.

A VALEDICTION: FORBIDDING MOURNING

As virtuous men pass mildly away,
And whisper to their souls, to go,
Whilst some of their sad friends do say,
The breath goes now, and some say, no:

So let us melt, and make no noise,
No tear-floods, nor sigh-tempests move,
'Twere profanation of our joys
To tell the laity our love.

Moving of th' earth brings harms and fears,
Men reckon what it did and meant,
But trepidation of the spheres,
Though greater far, is innocent.

Dull sublunary lovers' love
(Whose soul is sense) cannot admit
Absence, because it doth remove
Those things which elemented it.

But we by a love, so much refined,
That our selves know not what it is,
Inter-assured of the mind,
Care less, eyes, lips, and hands to miss.

Our two souls therefore, which are one,
Though I must go, endure not yet
A breach, but an expansion,
Like gold to aery thinness beat.

If they be two, they are two so
As stiff twin compasses are two,
Thy soul the fixed foot, makes no show
To move, but doth, if th'other do.

And though it in the centre sit,
   Yet when the other far doth roam,
It leans, and hearkens after it,
   And grows erect, as that comes home.

Such wilt thou be to me, who must
   Like th' other foot, obliquely run;
Thy firmness makes my circle just,
   And makes me end, where I begun.

WOMAN'S CONSTANCY

Now thou hast loved me one whole day,
Tomorrow when thou leav'st, what wilt thou say?
Wilt thou then antedate some new made vow?
  Or say that now
We are not just those persons, which we were?
Or, that oaths made in reverential fear
Of Love, and his wrath, any may forswear?
Or, as true deaths, true marriages untie,
So lovers' contracts, images of those,
Bind but till sleep, death's image, them unloose?
  Or, your own end to justify,
For having purposed change, and falsehood, you
Can have no way but falsehood to be true?
Vain lunatic, against these 'scapes I could
  Dispute, and conquer, if I would,
  Which I abstain to do,
For by tomorrow, I may think so too.

Divine Poems

LA CORONA

1

Deign at my hands this crown of prayer and praise,
Weaved in my low devout melancholy,
Thou which of good, hast, yea art treasury,
All changing unchanged Ancient of days,
But do not, with a vile crown of frail bays,
Reward my muse's white sincerity,
But what thy thorny crown gained, that give me,
A crown of glory, which doth flower always;
The ends crown our works, but thou crown'st our ends,
For, at our end begins our endless rest,
This first last end, now zealously possessed,
With a strong sober thirst, my soul attends.
'Tis time that heart and voice be lifted high,
Salvation to all that will is nigh.

2 Annunciation

Salvation to all that will is nigh,
That all, which always is all everywhere,
Which cannot sin, and yet all sins must bear,
Which cannot die, yet cannot choose but die,
Lo, faithful Virgin, yields himself to lie
In prison, in thy womb; and though he there
Can take no sin, nor thou give, yet he will wear
Taken from thence, flesh, which death's force may try.
Ere by the spheres time was created, thou
Wast in his mind, who is thy son, and brother,
Whom thou conceiv'st, conceived; yea thou art now
Thy maker's maker, and thy father's mother,
Thou hast light in dark; and shutt'st in little room,
Immensity cloistered in thy dear womb.

3 Nativity

Immensity cloistered in thy dear womb,
Now leaves his well-beloved imprisonment,
There he hath made himself to his intent
Weak enough, now into our world to come;
But oh, for thee, for him, hath th' inn no room?
Yet lay him in this stall, and from the orient,
Stars, and wisemen will travel to prevent
Th' effect of Herod's jealous general doom.
See'st thou, my soul, with thy faith's eyes, how he
Which fills all place, yet none holds him, doth lie?
Was not his pity towards thee wondrous high,
That would have need to be pitied by thee?
Kiss him, and with him into Egypt go,
With his kind mother, who partakes thy woe.

4 Temple

With his kind mother who partakes thy woe,
Joseph turn back; see where your child doth sit,
Blowing, yea blowing out those sparks of wit,
Which himself on the Doctors did bestow;
The Word but lately could not speak, and lo
It suddenly speaks wonders, whence comes it,
That all which was, and all which should be writ,
A shallow seeming child, should deeply know?
His godhead was not soul to his manhood,
Nor had time mellowed him to this ripeness,
But as for one which hath a long task, 'tis good,
With the sun to begin his business,
He in his age's morning thus began
By miracles exceeding power of man.

5 Crucifying

By miracles exceeding power of man,
He faith in some, envy in some begat,
For, what weak spirits admire, ambitious hate;
In both affections many to him ran,
But oh! the worst are most, they will and can,
Alas, and do, unto the immaculate,
Whose creature Fate is, now prescribe a fate,
Measuring self-life's infinity to a span,
Nay to an inch. Lo, where condemned he
Bears his own cross, with pain, yet by and by
When it bears him, he must bear more and die.
Now thou art lifted up, draw me to thee,
And at thy death giving such liberal dole,
Moist, with one drop of thy blood, my dry soul.

6 Resurrection

Moist with one drop of thy blood, my dry soul
Shall, (though she now be in extreme degree
Too stony hard, and yet too fleshly) be
Freed by that drop, from being starved, hard, or foul,
And life, by this death abled, shall control
Death, whom thy death slew; nor shall to me
Fear of first or last death, bring misery,
If in thy little book my name thou enrol,
Flesh in that long sleep is not putrefied,
But made that there, of which, and for which 'twas;
Nor can by other means be glorified.
May then sin's sleep, and death's soon from me pass,
That waked from both, I again risen may
Salute the last, and everlasting day.

7 Ascension

Salute the last and everlasting day,
Joy at the uprising of this sun, and son,
Ye whose just tears, or tribulation
Have purely washed, or burnt your drossy clay;
Behold the highest, parting hence away,
Lightens the dark clouds, which he treads upon,
Nor doth he by ascending, show alone,
But first he, and he first enters the way.
O strong ram, which hast battered heaven for me,
Mild lamb, which with thy blood, hast marked the path;
Bright torch, which shin'st, that I the way may see,
Oh, with thine own blood quench thine own just wrath,
And if thy holy Spirit, my Muse did raise,
Deign at my hands this crown of prayer and praise.

HOLY SONNETS

1

Thou hast made me, and shall thy work decay?
Repair me now, for now mine end doth haste,
I run to death, and death meets me as fast,
And all my pleasures are like yesterday,
I dare not move my dim eyes any way,
Despair behind, and death before doth cast
Such terror, and my feeble flesh doth waste
By sin in it, which it towards hell doth weigh;
Only thou art above, and when towards thee
By thy leave I can look, I rise again;
But our old subtle foe so tempteth me,
That not one hour I can myself sustain;
Thy Grace may wing me to prevent his art,
And thou like adamant draw mine iron heart.

2

As due by many titles I resign
Myself to thee, O God, first I was made
By thee, and for thee, and when I was decayed
Thy blood brought that, the which before was thine,
I am thy son, made with thy self to shine,
Thy servant, whose pains thou hast still repaid,
Thy sheep, thine image, and, till I betrayed
My self, a temple of thy Spirit divine;
Why doth the devil then usurp on me?
Why doth he steal, nay ravish that 's thy right?
Except thou rise and for thine own work fight,
Oh I shall soon despair, when I do see
That thou lov'st mankind well, yet wilt not choose me,
And Satan hates me, yet is loth to lose me.

3

O might those sighs and tears return again
Into my breast and eyes, which I have spent,
That I might in this holy discontent
Mourn with some fruit, as I have mourned in vain;
In mine idolatry what showers of rain
Mine eyes did waste! what griefs my heart did rent!
That sufferance was my sin, now I repent;
Because I did suffer I must suffer pain.
Th' hydroptic drunkard, and night-scouting thief,
The itchy lecher, and self tickling proud
Have the remembrance of past joys, for relief
Of coming ills. To poor me is allowed
No ease; for, long, yet vehement grief hath been
The effect and cause, the punishment and sin.

4

Oh my black soul! now thou art summoned
By sickness, death's herald, and champion;
Thou art like a pilgrim, which abroad hath done
Treason, and durst not turn to whence he is fled,
Or like a thief, which till death's doom be read,
Wisheth himself delivered from prison;
But damned and haled to execution,
Wisheth that still he might be imprisoned;
Yet grace, if thou repent, thou canst not lack;
But who shall give thee that grace to begin?
Oh make thyself with holy mourning black,
And red with blushing, as thou art with sin;
Or wash thee in Christ's blood, which hath this might
That being red, it dyes red souls to white.

5

I am a little world made cunningly
Of elements, and an angelic sprite,
But black sin hath betrayed to endless night
My world's both parts, and, oh, both parts must die.
You which beyond that heaven which was most high
Have found new spheres, and of new lands can write,
Pour new seas in mine eyes, that so I might
Drown my world with my weeping earnestly,
Or wash it if it must be drowned no more:
But oh it must be burnt; alas the fire
Of lust and envy have burnt it heretofore,
And made it fouler; let their flames retire,
And burn me O Lord, with a fiery zeal
Of thee and thy house, which doth in eating heal.

6

This is my play's last scene, here heavens appoint
My pilgrimage's last mile; and my race
Idly, yet quickly run, hath this last pace,
My span's last inch, my minute's latest point,
And gluttonous death, will instantly unjoint
My body, and soul, and I shall sleep a space,
But my ever-waking part shall see that face,
Whose fear already shakes my every joint:
Then, as my soul, to heaven her first seat, takes flight,
And earth-born body, in the earth shall dwell,
So, fall my sins, that all may have their right,
To where they are bred, and would press me, to hell.
Impute me righteous, thus purged of evil,
For thus I leave the world, the flesh, and devil.

7

At the round earth's imagined corners, blow
Your trumpets, angels, and arise, arise
From death, you numberless infinities
Of souls, and to your scattered bodies go,
All whom the flood did, and fire shall o'erthrow,
All whom war, dearth, age, agues, tyrannies,
Despair, law, chance, hath slain, and you whose eyes,
Shall behold God, and never taste death's woe.
But let them sleep, Lord, and me mourn a space,
For, if above all these, my sins abound,
'Tis late to ask abundance of thy grace,
When we are there; here on this lowly ground,
Teach me how to repent; for that's as good
As if thou hadst sealed my pardon, with thy blood.

8

If faithful souls be alike glorified
As angels, then my father's soul doth see,
And adds this even to full felicity,
That valiantly I hell's wide mouth o'erstride:
But if our minds to these souls be descried
By circumstances, and by signs that be
Apparent in us, not immediately,
How shall my mind's white truth by them be tried?
They see idolatrous lovers weep and mourn,
And vile blasphemous conjurers to call
On Jesus' name, and pharisaical
Dissemblers feign devotion. Then turn
O pensive soul, to God, for he knows best
Thy true grief, for he put it in my breast.

9

If poisonous minerals, and if that tree,
Whose fruit threw death on else immortal us,
If lecherous goats, if serpents envious
Cannot be damned; alas, why should I be?
Why should intent or reason, born in me,
Make sins, else equal, in me more heinous?
And mercy being easy, and glorious
To God, in his stern wrath, why threatens he?
But who am I, that dare dispute with thee
O God? Oh! of thine only worthy blood,
And my tears, make a heavenly lethean flood,
And drown in it my sin's black memory;
That thou remember them, some claim as debt,
I think it mercy, if thou wilt forget.

10

Death be not proud, though some have called thee
Mighty and dreadful, for, thou art not so,
For, those, whom thou think'st, thou dost overthrow,
Die not, poor death, nor yet canst thou kill me;
From rest and sleep, which but thy pictures be,
Much pleasure, then from thee, much more must flow,
And soonest our best men with thee do go,
Rest of their bones, and soul's delivery.
Thou art slave to fate, chance, kings, and desperate men,
And dost with poison, war, and sickness dwell,
And poppy, or charms can make us sleep as well,
And better than thy stroke; why swell'st thou then?
One short sleep past, we wake eternally,
And death shall be no more, Death thou shalt die.

11

Spit in my face ye Jews, and pierce my side,
Buffet, and scoff, scourge, and crucify me,
For I have sinned, and sinned, and only he,
Who could do no iniquity, hath died:
But by my death can not be satisfied
My sins, which pass the Jews' impiety:
They killed once an inglorious man, but I
Crucify him daily, being now glorified.
Oh let me then, his strange love still admire:
Kings pardon, but he bore our punishment.
And Jacob came clothed in vile harsh attire
But to supplant, and with gainful intent:
God clothed himself in vile man's flesh, that so
He might be weak enough to suffer woe.

12

Why are we by all creatures waited on?
Why do the prodigal elements supply
Life and food to me, being more pure than I,
Simple, and further from corruption?
Why brook'st thou, ignorant horse, subjection?
Why dost thou bull, and boar so sillily
Dissemble weakness, and by one man's stroke die,
Whose whole kind, you might swallow and feed upon?
Weaker I am, woe is me, and worse than you,
You have not sinned, nor need be timorous.
But wonder at a greater wonder, for to us
Created nature doth these things subdue,
But their Creator, whom sin, nor nature tied,
For us, his creatures, and his foes, hath died.

13

What if this present were the world's last night?
Mark in my heart, O soul, where thou dost dwell,
The picture of Christ crucified, and tell
Whether that countenance can thee affright,
Tears in his eyes quench the amazing light,
Blood fills his frowns, which from his pierced head fell,
And can that tongue adjudge thee unto hell,
Which prayed forgiveness for his foes' fierce spite?
No, no; but as in my idolatry
I said to all my profane mistresses,
Beauty, of pity, foulness only is
A sign of rigour: so I say to thee,
To wicked spirits are horrid shapes assigned,
This beauteous form assures a piteous mind.

14

Batter my heart, three-personed God; for, you
As yet but knock, breathe, shine, and seek to mend;
That I may rise, and stand, o'erthrow me, and bend
Your force, to break, blow, burn, and make me new.
I, like an usurped town, to another due,
Labour to admit you, but oh, to no end,
Reason your viceroy in me, me should defend,
But is captived, and proves weak or untrue,
Yet dearly I love you, and would be loved fain,
But am betrothed unto your enemy,
Divorce me, untie, or break that knot again,
Take me to you, imprison me, for I
Except you enthral me, never shall be free,
Nor ever chaste, except you ravish me.

15

Wilt thou love God, as he thee? then digest,
My soul, this wholesome meditation,
How God the Spirit, by angels waited on
In heaven, doth make his temple in thy breast.
The Father having begot a Son most blessed,
And still begetting, (for he ne'er begun)
Hath deigned to choose thee by adoption,
Coheir to his glory, and Sabbath's endless rest;
And as a robbed man, which by search doth find
His stol'n stuff sold, must lose or buy it again:
The Son of glory came down, and was slain,
Us whom he had made, and Satan stol'n, to unbind.
'Twas much, that man was made like God before,
But, that God should be made like man, much more.

16

Father, part of his double interest
Unto thy kingdom, thy Son gives to me,
His jointure in the knotty Trinity
He keeps, and gives me his death's conquest.
This Lamb, whose death, with life the world hath blessed,
Was from the world's beginning slain, and he
Hath made two wills, which with the legacy
Of his and thy kingdom, do thy sons invest.
Yet such are thy laws, that men argue yet
Whether a man those statutes can fulfil;
None doth, but thy all-healing grace and Spirit
Revive again what law and letter kill.
Thy law's abridgement, and thy last command
Is all but love; oh let that last will stand!

17

Since she whom I loved hath paid her last debt
To nature, and to hers, and my good is dead,
And her soul early into heaven ravished,
Wholly in heavenly things my mind is set.
Here the admiring her my mind did whet
To seek thee God; so streams do show the head,
But though I have found thee, and thou my thirst hast fed,
A holy thirsty dropsy melts me yet.
But why should I beg more love, when as thou
Dost woo my soul for hers; offering all thine:
And dost not only fear lest I allow
My love to saints and angels, things divine,
But in thy tender jealousy dost doubt
Lest the world, flesh, yea Devil put thee out.

18

Show me dear Christ, thy spouse, so bright and clear.
What, is it she, which on the other shore
Goes richly painted? or which robbed and tore
Laments and mourns in Germany and here?
Sleeps she a thousand, then peeps up one year?
Is she self truth and errs? now new, now outwore?
Doth she, and did she, and shall she evermore
On one, on seven, or on no hill appear?
Dwells she with us, or like adventuring knights
First travail we to seek and then make love?
Betray kind husband thy spouse to our sights,
And let mine amorous soul court thy mild dove,
Who is most true, and pleasing to thee, then
When she is embraced and open to most men.

19

Oh, to vex me, contraries meet in one:
Inconstancy unnaturally hath begot
A constant habit; that when I would not
I change in vows, and in devotion.
As humorous is my contrition
As my profane love, and as soon forgot:
As riddlingly distempered, cold and hot,
As praying, as mute; as infinite, as none.
I durst not view heaven yesterday; and today
In prayers, and flattering speeches I court God:
Tomorrow I quake with true fear of his rod.
So my devout fits come and go away
Like a fantastic ague: save that here
Those are my best days, when I shake with fear.

UPON THE ANNUNCIATION AND PASSION FALLING UPON ONE DAY. 1608

Tamely frail body abstain today; today
My soul eats twice, Christ hither and away.
She sees him man, so like God made in this,
That of them both a circle emblem is,
Whose first and last concur; this doubtful day
Of feast or fast, Christ came, and went away;
She sees him nothing twice at once, who is all;
She sees a cedar plant itself, and fall,
Her maker put to making, and the head
Of life, at once, not yet alive, and dead;
She sees at once the virgin mother stay
Reclused at home, public at Golgotha.
Sad and rejoiced she's seen at once, and seen
At almost fifty, and at scarce fifteen.
At once a son is promised her, and gone,
Gabriel gives Christ to her, he her to John;
Not fully a mother, she's in orbity,
At once receiver and the legacy;
All this, and all between, this day hath shown,
Th' abridgement of Christ's story, which makes one
(As in plain maps, the furthest west is east)
Of the angels' Ave, and Consummatum est.
How well the Church, God's court of faculties
Deals, in some times, and seldom joining these;
As by the self-fixed pole we never do
Direct our course, but the next star thereto,
Which shows where the'other is, and which we say
(Because it strays not far) doth never stray;
So God by his Church, nearest to him, we know,
And stand firm, if we by her motion go;
His Spirit, as his fiery pillar doth
Lead, and his Church, as cloud; to one end both:
This Church, by letting these days join, hath shown

Death and conception in mankind is one.
Or 'twas in him the same humility,
That he would be a man, and leave to be:
Or as creation he had made, as God,
With the last judgement, but one period,
His imitating spouse would join in one
Manhood's extremes: he shall come, he is gone:
Or as though one blood drop, which thence did fall,
Accepted, would have served, he yet shed all;
So though the least of his pains, deeds, or words,
Would busy a life, she all this day affords;
This treasure then, in gross, my soul uplay,
And in my life retail it every day.

GOOD FRIDAY, 1613. RIDING WESTWARD

Let man's soul be a sphere, and then, in this,
The intelligence that moves, devotion is,
And as the other spheres, by being grown
Subject to foreign motions, lose their own,
And being by others hurried every day,
Scarce in a year their natural form obey:
Pleasure or business, so, our souls admit
For their first mover, and are whirled by it.
Hence is't, that I am carried towards the west
This day, when my soul's form bends toward the east.
There I should see a sun, by rising set,
And by that setting endless day beget;
But that Christ on this Cross, did rise and fall,
Sin had eternally benighted all.
Yet dare I almost be glad, I do not see
That spectacle of too much weight for me.
Who sees God's face, that is self life, must die;
What a death were it then to see God die?
It made his own lieutenant Nature shrink,
It made his footstool crack, and the sun wink.
Could I behold those hands which span the poles,
And turn all spheres at once, pierced with those holes?
Could I behold that endless height which is
Zenith to us, and to our antipodes,
Humbled below us? or that blood which is
The seat of all our souls, if not of his,
Made dirt of dust, or that flesh which was worn,
By God, for his apparel, ragged, and torn?
If on these things I durst not look, durst I
Upon his miserable mother cast mine eye,
Who was God's partner here, and furnished thus
Half of that sacrifice, which ransomed us?
Though these things, as I ride, be from mine eye,
They are present yet unto my memory,

For that looks towards them; and thou look'st
towards me,
O Saviour, as thou hang'st upon the tree;
I turn my back to thee, but to receive
Corrections, till thy mercies bid thee leave.
O think me worth thine anger, punish me,
Burn off my rusts, and my deformity,
Restore thine image, so much, by thy grace,
That thou mayst know me, and I'll turn my face.

TO MR TILMAN AFTER HE HAD TAKEN ORDERS

Thou, those diviner soul hath caused thee now
To put thy hand unto the holy plough,
Making lay-scornings of the Ministry,
Not an impediment, but victory;
What bringst thou home with thee? how is thy mind
Affected in the vintage? Dost thou find
New thoughts and stirrings in thee? and as steel
Touched with a loadstone, dost new motions feel?
Or, as a ship after much pain and care,
For iron and cloth brings home rich Indian ware,
Hast thou thus trafficked, but with far more gain
Of noble goods, and with less time and pain?
Art thou the same materials, as before,
Only the stamp is changed; but no more?
And as new crowned kings alter the face,
But not the money's substance; so hath grace
Changed only God's old image by creation,
To Christ's new stamp, at this thy coronation?
Or, as we paint angels with wings, because
They bear God's message, and proclaim his laws,
Since thou must do the like, and so must move,
Art thou new feathered with celestial love?
Dear, tell me where thy purchase lies, and show
What thy advantage is above, below.
But if thy gaining do surmount expression,
Why doth the foolish world scorn that profession,
Whose joys pass speech? Why do they think unfit
That gentry should join families with it?
As if their day were only to be spent
In dressing, mistressing and compliment;
Alas poor joys, but poorer men, whose trust
Seems richly placed in refined dust;
(For, such are clothes and beauty, which though gay,
Are, at the best, but as sublimed clay.)

Let then the world thy calling disrespect,
But go thou on, and pity their neglect.
What function is so noble, as to be
Ambassador to God and destiny?
To open life, to give kingdoms to more
Than kings give dignities; to keep heaven's door?
Mary's prerogative was to bear Christ, so
'Tis preachers' to convey him, for they do
As angels out of clouds, from pulpits speak;
And bless the poor beneath, the lame, the weak.
If then th' astronomers, whereas they spy
A new-found star, their optics magnify,
How brave are those, who with their engines, can
Bring man to heaven, and heaven again to man?
These are thy titles and pre-eminences,
In whom must meet God's graces, men's offences,
And so the heavens which beget all things here,
And the earth our mother, which these things doth bear,
Both these in thee, are in thy calling knit,
And make thee now a blessed hermaphrodite.

A HYMN TO CHRIST, AT THE AUTHOR'S LAST GOING INTO GERMANY

In what torn ship soever I embark,
That ship shall be my emblem of thy ark;
What sea soever swallow me, that flood
Shall be to me an emblem of thy blood;
Though thou with clouds of anger do disguise
Thy face; yet through that mask I know those eyes,
Which, though they turn away sometimes,
They never will despise.

I sacrifice this Island unto thee,
And all whom I loved there, and who loved me;
When I have put our seas twixt them and me,
Put thou thy sea betwixt my sins and thee.
As the tree's sap doth seek the root below
In winter, in my winter now I go,
Where none but thee, th' eternal root
Of true love I may know.

Nor thou nor thy religion dost control,
The amorousness of an harmonious soul,
But thou wouldst have that love thyself: as thou
Art jealous, Lord, so I am jealous now,
Thou lov'st not, till from loving more, thou free
My soul; who ever gives, takes liberty:
O, if thou car'st not whom I love
Alas, thou lov'st not me.

Seal then this bill of my divorce to all,
On whom those fainter beams of love did fall;
Marry those loves, which in youth scattered be
On fame, wit, hopes (false mistresses) to thee.
Churches are best for prayer, that have least light:
To see God only, I go out of sight:
And to 'scape stormy days, I choose
An everlasting night.

HYMN TO GOD MY GOD, IN MY SICKNESS

Since I am coming to that holy room,
  Where, with thy choir of saints for evermore,
I shall be made thy music; as I come
  I tune the instrument here at the door,
  And what I must do then, think here before.

Whilst my physicians by their love are grown
  Cosmographers, and I their map, who lie
Flat on this bed, that by them may be shown
  That this is my south-west discovery
  Per fretum febris, by these straits to die.

I joy, that in these straits, I see my west;
  For, though their currents yield return to none,
What shall my west hurt me? As west and east
  In all flat maps (and I am one) are one,
  So death doth touch the resurrection.

Is the Pacific Sea my home? Or are
  The eastern riches? Is Jerusalem?
Anyan, and Magellan, and Gibraltar,
  All straits, and none but straits, are ways to them,
  Whether where Japhet dwelt, or Cham, or Shem.

We think that Paradise and Calvary,
  Christ's Cross, and Adam's tree, stood in one place;
Look Lord, and find both Adams met in me;
  As the first Adam's sweat surrounds my face,
  May the last Adam's blood my soul embrace.

So, in his purple wrapped receive me Lord,
  By these his thorns give me his other crown;
And as to others' souls I preached thy word,
  Be this my text, my sermon to mine own,
  Therefore that he may raise the Lord throws down.

A HYMN TO GOD THE FATHER

Wilt thou forgive that sin where I begun,
Which was my sin, though it were done before?
Wilt thou forgive that sin, through which I run,
And do run still: though still I do deplore?
When thou hast done, thou hast not done,
For, I have more.

Wilt thou forgive that sin which I have won
Others to sin? and, made my sin their door?
Wilt thou forgive that sin which I did shun
A year, or two: but wallowed in, a score?
When thou hast done, thou hast not done,
For I have more.

I have a sin of fear, that when I have spun
My last thread, I shall perish on the shore;
But swear by thy self, that at my death thy son
Shall shine as he shines now, and heretofore;
And, having done that, thou hast done,
I fear no more.

Sermons

CHRIST THE LIGHT

He was not that light, but was sent to bear witness of that light.
John 1:8

Who Is This Light?

Though most expositors, as well ancient as modern, agree with one general and unanimous consent that light in this verse is intended and meant of Christ; Christ is this light, yet in some precedent and subsequent passages in this chapter I see other senses have been admitted of this word, light, than perchance those places will bear; certainly other than those places need; particularly in the fourth verse ('In it was life, and that life was the light of men') there they understand 'life' to be nothing but this natural life which we breath, and 'light' to be only that natural light, natural reason, which distinguishes us men from other creatures. Now it is true that they may have a pretence for some ground of this interpretation in antiquity itself, for, so says Saint Cyril,

'Christ doth enlighten us in creating us'. And so some others of the Fathers and some of the Schools, understand by that light natural reason and that life, conservation in life. But this interpretation seems to me subject to both these dangers, that it goes so far and yet reaches not home. So far in wresting in divers senses into a word which needs but one and is of itself clear enough, that is 'light'; and yet reaches not home, for it reaches not to the essential light which is Christ Jesus, nor to the supernatural light which is faith and grace, which seems to have been the evangelist's principal scope, to declare the coming of Christ (who is the essential light) and his purpose in coming, to raise and establish a Church, by faith and grace, which is the supernatural light. For as the Holy Ghost himself interprets life to be meant of Christ ('He that hath the Son hath life'), so we may justly do of light too ('He that sees' the Son, the 'Son of God hath light'). For light is never (to my remembrance) found in any place of the Scripture where it must necessarily signify the light of nature, natural reason; but wheresoever it is transferred from the natural to a figurative sense, it takes a higher signification than 'that'. Either it signifies essential light, Christ Jesus (which answers our first question, 'Who is this light,' it is Christ, personally) or it signifies the supernatural light of faith and grace (which answers our second question, 'What is this light,' for it is the working of Christ by his Spirit in his Church, in the infusion of faith and grace, for belief and manners). And therefore though it be ever lawful, and oftentimes very useful, for the raising and exaltation of our devotion, and to present the plenty and abundance of the Holy Ghost in the Scriptures, who satisfies us as with marrow and with fatness, to induce the diverse senses that the Scriptures do admit; yet this may not be admitted, if there may be danger thereby, to neglect or weaken the literal sense itself. For there is no necessity of that spiritual wantonness of finding more than necessary senses; for the more lights there are the more shadows are also cast by those many lights. And, as it is true in religious duties, so is it in interpretation of matters of religion; when you have done that you ought to do in your calling, you have done enough. There are no such evangelical counsels as should raise works of supererogation, more then you are bound to do, so when you have the necessary sense, that is the meaning of the Holy Ghost in that place, you have senses enough, and not till then, though you have never so many and never so delightful.

That Light

Light, therefore, is in all this chapter fitliest understood of Christ, who is noted here with that distinctive article, 'that light'. For Christ is not so called 'Light' as he is called a 'Rock', or a 'Cornerstone', not by a metaphor, but truly and properly. It is true that the Apostles are said to be light, and that with an article 'the light'; but yet with a limitation and restriction, 'the light of the world', that is, set up to convey light to the world. It is true that John Baptist himself was called 'light', and with large additions 'a burning, and a shining lamp', to denote both his own burning zeal and the communicating of this his light to others. It is true that 'all the faithful' are said to be 'light in the Lord'. But all this is but to signify that they had been in darkness before; they had been beclouded but were now illustrated; they were light, but light by reflection, by illustration of a greater light. And in the first creation, 'The evening and the morning made the day, evening' before 'morning, darkness' before 'light', so in our regeneration, when we are made new creatures, the Spirit of God finds us in natural darkness, and by him we are made light in the Lord. But Christ himself, and he only, is 'that light, the true light'. Not so opposed to those other lights as though the Apostles, or John Baptist, or the faithful, who are called lights, were false lights; but that they were weak lights. But Christ was 'the fountain of all light'; light so, as nobody else was so.

All other men, by occasion of this flesh, have dark clouds, yea nights, yea long and frozen winter nights of sin, and of the works of darkness. Christ was incapable of any such nights or any such clouds, any approaches toward sin. But yet Christ admitted some shadows, some such degrees of human infirmity, as by them, he was willing to show that the nature of man, in the best perfection thereof, is not 'true light, all light', which he declared in that 'If it be possible, let this cup pass'; words to which himself was pleased to allow so much of a retraction and a correction, 'yet Father,' whatsoever the sadness of my soul have made me say, 'yet not my will but thine be done; not mine, but thine'; so that they were not altogether all one; human infirmity made some difference. So that no one man, not Christ (considered but as a man), was 'all light,' no cloud. No not mankind, consider it collectively, can be light so as that there shall be no darkness.

Nay not only no man (for so we may consider him in the whole course of his life), but no one act of the most perfect and religious man in the world, though that act employ but half a minute in the doing thereof can be 'true light', all light, so perfect light, as that it may serve another, or thyself, for a lantern to his or thy feet, or a light to his or thy steps, so that he or thou may think it enough to do so still. For another man may do so good works as it may justly work to thy shame and confusion, and to the aggravating of thy condemnation, that thou livest not as well as he, yet it would not perchance serve thy turn to live but so well; for 'to whom God gives more, of him he requires more'.

Natural Light

In all philosophy there is not so dark a thing as light. As the sun, which is the beginning of natural light, is the most evident thing to be seen and yet the hardest to be looked upon, so is natural light to our reason and understanding. Nothing clearer, for it is clearness itself; nothing darker, it is enwrapped in so many scruples. Nothing nearer, for it is round about us; nothing more remote, for we know neither entrance nor limits of it. Nothing more easy, for a child discerns it; nothing more hard, for no man understands it. It is apprehensible by sense and not comprehensible by reason. If we wink, we cannot choose but see it; if we stare, we know it never the better. No man is yet got so near to the knowledge of the qualities of light as to know whether light itself be a quality or a substance. If then this natural light be so dark to our natural reason, if we shall offer to pierce so far into the light, of this text, the essential light Christ Jesus (in his nature, or but in his offices), or the supernatural light of faith and grace (how far faith may be had and yet lost, and how far the free will of man may concur and cooperate with grace, and yet still remain nothing in itself), if we search farther into these points, then the Scripture hath opened us a way, how shall we hope to unentangle or extricate ourselves? They had a precious composition for lamps amongst the ancients, reserved especially for tombs, which kept light for many hundreds of years; we have had in our age experience in some casual openings of ancient vaults of finding such lights as were kindled (as appeared by their inscription) fifteen or sixteen hundred years before; but as soon as that light comes to our light it vanishes.

So this eternal and this supernatural light, Christ and faith, enlightens, warms, purges, and does all the profitable offices of fire and light, if we keep it in the right sphere, in the proper place (that is, if we consist in points necessary to salvation and revealed in the Scripture) but when we bring this light to the common light of reason, to our inferences, and consequences, it may be in danger to vanish itself and perchance extinguish our reason too. We may search so far and reason so long of faith and grace as that we may lose not only them but even our reason too, and sooner become mad than good. Not that we are bound to believe anything against reason, that is to believe we know not why. It is but a slack opinion, it is not belief, that is not grounded upon reason.

He that should come to a heathen man, a mere natural man, uncatechized, uninstructed in the rudiments of the Christian religion, and should at first, without any preparation, present him first with this necessity: Thou shalt burn in fire and brimstone eternally except thou believe in a Trinity of persons, in an unity of one God, except thou believe the Incarnation of the second person of the Trinity, the Son of God, except thou believe that a virgin had a son and the same Son that God had, and that God was man too and being the immortal God yet died, he should be so far from working any spiritual cure upon this poor soul, as that he should rather bring Christian mysteries into scorn than him to a belief. For that man, if you proceed so (believe all or you burn in hell), would find an easy, an obvious way to escape all; that is, first not to believe in hell itself, and then nothing could bind him to believe the rest.

The reason therefore of man, must first be satisfied; but the way of such satisfaction must be this, to make him see, that this World, a frame of so much harmony, so much concinnity and conveniencey, and such a correspondence and subordination in the parts thereof, must necessarily have had a workman, for nothing can make itself: that no such workman would deliver over a frame and work of so much majesty to be governed by fortune, casually, but would still retain the administration thereof in his own hands; that if he do so, if he made the world and sustain it still by his watchful providence, there belongeth a worship and service to him for doing so; that therefore he hath certainly revealed to man what kind of worship and service shall be acceptable to him; that this manifestation of his will must be permanent, it must be written, there must be a Scripture, which is his Word and his Will; and that therefore from the Scripture, from that Word of God, all articles of our belief are to be drawn.

If then his reason confessing all this ask for further proof, how he shall know that these Scriptures accepted by the Christian Church are the true Scriptures, let him bring any other book which pretendeth to be the Word of God into comparison with these. It is true, we have not a demonstration; not such an evidence as that one and two are three, to prove these to be the Scriptures of God; God hath not proceeded in that manner to drive our reason into a pound and to force it by peremptory necessity to accept these for Scriptures, for then here had been no exercise of our will and our assent, if we could not have resisted. But yet these Scriptures have so orderly, so sweet and so powerful a working upon the reason and the understanding, as if any third man, who were utterly discharged of all preconceptions and anticipations in matter of religion, one who were altogether neutral, disinterested, unconcerned in either part, he would be drawn to such an historical, such a grammatical, such a logical belief of our Bible as to prefer it before any other that could be pretended to be the Word of God. He would believe it and he would know why he did so. For let no man think that God hath given him so much ease here as to save him by believing he knoweth not what, or why.

The Light of Essence and the Light of Glory

We shall consider some few couples; and the first pair, the light of the essence of God and the light of the glory of his Saints. And though the first of these be that essential light by which we shall see God face to face, as he is, and the effluence and emanation of beams from the face of God, which make that place heaven, of which light it is said, 'That God who only hath immortality, dwells in light inaccessible in the light that none can attain to; yet by the light of faith and grace in sanctification we may come to such a participation of that light of essence, or such a reflection of it in this world, that it shall be true of us which was said of those Ephesians, 'You were once darkness, but now are light in the Lord'; he does not say 'enlightened', nor 'lightsome', but light itself, light essentially, for our conversation is in heaven. And as God says of Jerusalem, and his blessings here in this world, 'I have shod thee with badgers skin' (which the ancients take for some precious stuff), that is, I have enabled thee to tread upon all the most estimable things of this world . . . so the 'precious promises of Christ, make us partakers of the divine nature', and the light of faith makes us the same 'Spirit with the Lord'. And this is our participation of the light of essence in this life. The next is the light of glory.

This is that glorification which we shall have at the last day of which glory we consider a great part to be in that denudation, that manifestation of all to all. In this world, a great part of our inglorious servitude is in those disguises, and palliations, those colours and pretences of public good with which men of power and authority apparel their oppressions of the poor; in this are we the more miserable, that we cannot see their ends, that there is none of this denudation, this laying open of ourselves to one another, which shall accompany that state of glory, where we shall see one another's bodies and souls, actions and thoughts. And therefore, as if this place were now that tribunal of Christ Jesus, and this that day of judgement and denudation, we must be here, as we shall be there, content to stand naked before him; content that there be a discovery, a revealing, a manifestation of all our sins, wrought upon us, at least to our own consciences, though not to the congregation. If we will have glory, we must have this denudation.

We must not be glad when our sins scape the preacher. We must not say (as though there were a comfort in that), though he have hit such a man's adultery, and another's ambition, and another's extortion, yet, for all his diligence, he hath missed my sin; for if thou wouldest fain have it missed, thou wouldest fain hold it still. And then, why camest thou hither? What camest thou for to church, or to the sacrament? Why doest thou delude God with this complemental visit, to come to his house, if thou bring not with thee a disposition to his honour and his service? Camest thou only to try whether God knew the sin and could tell thee of it by the preacher? Alas, he knows it infallibly; and, if he take no knowledge of his knowing it, to thy conscience, by the words of the preacher, thy state is the more desperate.

God sends us to preach forgiveness of sins; where we find no sin we have no commission to execute. How shall we find your sins? In the old sacrifices of the law the priest did not fetch the sacrifice from the herd, but he received it from him that brought it, and so sacrificed it for him. Do thou therefore prevent the preacher? Accuse thyself before he accuse thee; offer up thy sin thyself; bring it to the top of thy memory and thy conscience, that he finding it there may sacrifice for thee. Tune the instrument, and it is the fitter for his hand. Remember thou thine own sins first, and then every word that falls from the preacher's lips shall be a drop of the dew of heaven, dram of the 'balm of Gilead', a portion of the blood of thy Saviour, to wash away that sin, so presented by thee to be so sacrificed by him.

This then is our first couple of these lights. By our conversation in heaven here (that is, a watchfulness that we fall not into sin) we have possession and fruition of heaven, and of the light of God's essence. And then, if we do, by infirmity, fall into sin, yet by this denudation of our souls, this manifestation of our sins to God by confession, and to that purpose a gladness when we hear our sins spoken of by the preacher, we have the light of glory, and inchoation of our glorified estate.

The Light of Faith and the Light of Nature

Of these two lights, faith and grace, first, and then nature and reason, we said something before, but never so much because contentious spirits have cast such clouds upon both these lights that some have said, nature doth all alone, and other, that nature hath nothing to do at all, but all is grace. We decline wranglings that tend not to edification; we say only to our present purpose (which is the operation of these several couples of lights) that by this light of faith, to him that hath it, all that is involved in prophecies is clear and evident, as in a history already done; and all that is wrapped up in promises is his own already in performance. That man needs not go so high for his assurance of a Messiah and Redeemer, as to the first promise made to him in Adam; nor for the limitation of the stock and race from whence this Messiah should come, so far as to the renewing of this promise in Abraham; nor for the description of this Messiah, who he should be and of whom he should be born, as to Isaiah; nor to Micah for the place; nor for the time when he should accomplish all this, so far as to Daniel; no, nor so far as to the evangelists themselves for the history and the evidence that all this that was done in his behalf by the Messiah was done 1600 years since. But he hath a whole Bible and an abundant library in his own heart, and there by this light of faith (which is not only a knowing, but an applying, an appropriating of all to thy benefit) he hath a better knowledge than all this, than either prophetical or evangelical, for though both these be irrefragable and infallible proofs of a Messiah, yet both these might but concern others. His light of faith brings him home to thee.

How sure so ever I be that the world shall never perish by water, yet I may be drowned; and how sure so ever that the 'Lamb of God hath taken away the sins of the world'. I may perish without I have this applicatory faith. And as he needs not look back to Isaiah, nor Abraham, nor Adam, for the Messiah, so neither needs he to look forward. He needs not stay in expectation of the Angels' trumpets to awaken the dead; he is not put to his Lord, 'How long, Lord, wilt thou defer our restitution?' He hath already 'died the death of the righteous', which is to die to sin; he hath already had his burial by being buried with Christ in Baptism; he hath had his resurrection from sin, his ascension to holy purposes of amendment of life, and his judgement, that is, 'peace of conscience', sealed unto him; and so by this light of applying faith, he hath already apprehended an eternal possession of God's eternal kingdom. This, though a fainter light, directs us to the other, nature to faith. And as by the quantity in the light of the moon we know the position and distance of the sun, how far or how near the sun is to her, so by the working of the light of nature in us we may discern (by the measure and virtue and heat of that) how near to the other greater light, the light of faith, we stand. If we find our natural faculties rectified so as that free will which we have in moral and civil actions be bent upon the external duties of religion (as ever natural man may, out of the use of that free will, come to church, hear the Word preached, and believe it to be true), we may be sure the other greater light is about us. If we be cold in them, in actuating, in exalting, in using our natural faculties so far, we shall be deprived of all light; we shall not see the invisible God in visible things, which Saint Paul makes so inexcusable, so unpardonable a thing; we shall not see the hand of God in all our worldly crosses, nor the seal of God in all our worldly blessings; we shall not see the face of God in his house, his presence here in the church, nor the mind of God in his Gospel, that his gracious purposes upon mankind extend so particularly, or reach so far, as to include us.

I shall hear in the Scripture his 'Come all', and yet I shall think that his eye was not upon me, that his eye did not beckon me and I shall hear that 'God would save all'; yet I shall find some perverse reason in myself, why it is not likely that God will save me. I am commanded 'to search the Scriptures', now that is not to be able to repeat any history of the Bible without book, it is not to ruffle a Bible, and upon any word to turn to the chapter and to the verse; but this is the true searching of the Scriptures, to find all the histories to be examples to me, all the prophecies to induce a Saviour for me, all the Gospel to apply Christ Jesus to me.

Turn over all the folds and plaits of thine own heart and find there the infirmities and waverings of thine own faith, and an ability to say, 'Lord I believe, help mine unbelief'; and then, though thou have no Bible in thy hand, or though thou stand in a dark corner, nay though thou canst not read a letter, thou hast searched that Scripture, thou hast turned to Mark 9:24. Turn thine ear to God, and hear him turning to thee, and saying to thy soul, 'I will marry thee to myself forever'; and thou hast searched the Scripture and turned to Hosea 2:19. Turn to thine own history, thine own life, and if thou canst read there that thou hast endeavoured to turn thine ignorance into knowledge and thy knowledge into practice, if thou find thyself to be an example of that rule of Christ's, 'If you know these things, blessed are you if you do them'; then thou hast searched that Scripture and turned to John 13:17. This is 'to search the Scriptures', not as though thou wouldest make a concordance, but an application; as thou wouldest search a wardrobe not to make an inventory of it, but to find in it something fit for thy wearing.

John Baptist was not the light, he was not Christ, but 'he bore witness of him'. The light of faith, in the highest exaltation that can be had in the elect, here, is not that very 'beautific vision' which we shall have in heaven, but it bears witness to that light. The light of nature in the highest exaltation is not faith, but it bears witness of it. The lights of faith and of nature are subordinate John Baptists: faith bears me witness that I have Christ, and the light of nature, that is the exalting of my natural faculties towards religious uses, bears me witness that I have faith. Only that man whose conscience testifies to himself, and whose actions testify to the world that he does what he can, can believe himself, or be believed by others, that he had the true light of faith.

And therefore, as the Apostle saith, 'Quench not the Spirit'; I say too, 'Quench not the light of nature', suffer not that light to go out; study your natural faculties; husband and improve them, and love the outward acts of religion, though an hypocrite and though a natural man may do them. Certainly he that loves not the militant church, hath but a faint faith in his interest in the triumphant. He that cares not though the material church fall, I am afraid is falling from the spiritual. For can a man be sure to have his money, or his plate, if his house be burnt? or to preserve his faith, if the outward exercises of religion fail? He that undervalues outward things in the religious service of God, though he begin at ceremonial and ritual things, will come quickly to call sacraments but outward things, and sermons and public prayers but outward things, in contempt. The bell that calls me to church does not catechize me, nor preach to me; yet I observe the sound of that bell, because it brings me to him that does those offices to me. The light of nature is far from being enough; but, as a candle may kindle a torch, so into the faculties of nature, well employed, God infuses faith.

The Light of Heavenly Bodies and the Light of Fire

And a third pair of lights of attestation, that bear witness to the light of our text, is the light which the sun and moon, and those glorious bodies give from heaven, and the light which those things that are naturally combustible and apt to take fire, do give upon earth, both these bear witness of this light, that is, admit an application to it. For, in the first of these, the glorious lights of heaven, we must take nothing for stars that are not stars; nor make astrological and fixed conclusions out of meteors that are but transitory; they may be comets, and blazing stars, and so portend much mischief, but they are not fixed stars, not stars of heaven. As in the heavens the stars were created at once, with one fiat and then being so made, stars do not beget new stars, so the Christian doctrine necessary to salvation was delivered at once, that is, entirely in one sphere, in the body of the Scriptures. And then, as stars do not beget stars, articles of faith do not beget articles of faith. 'Other foundation can no man lay than Christ': not only no better, but no other; what other things soever are added by men, enter not into the nature and condition of a foundation.

Now for the consideration of the other light of this third couple, which is the light of fire, the light of things which take and give light here upon earth. If we reduce it to application and practise, and contract it to one instance, it will appear that the devotion and zeal of him that is best affected, is, for the most part, in the disposition of a torch, or a knife, ordained to take fire and to give light. If it have never been lightened, it does not easily take light, but it must be bruised and beaten first; if it have been lighted and put out, though it cannot take fire of itself, yet it does easily conceive fire if it be presented within any convenient distance. Such also is the soul of man towards the finest of the zeal of God's glory, and compassion of other's misery. If there be any that never took this fire, that was never affected with either of these, the glory of God, the miseries of other men, can I hope to kindle him? It must be God's work to bruise and beat him with his rod of affliction, before he will take fire.

But for you who have taken this fire before, that have been enlightened in both sacraments, and in the preaching of the word; in the means and in some measure of practise of holiness heretofore; if in supplying oil to your lamps, which God by his ordinance had kindled in you, you have let this light go out by negligence or inconsideration, or that storms of worldly calamities have blown it out, do but now at this instant call to mind what sin of yesterday, or t'other day, or long ago, begun, and practised, and prevailed upon you, or what future sin, what purpose of doing a sin tonight, or tomorrow, possesses you. Do but think seriously what sin or what cross hath blown out that light, that grace, which was formerly in you, before that sin or that cross invaded you, and turn your soul, which hath been enlightened before, towards this fire which God's Spirit blows this minute, and you will conceive new fire, new zeal, new compassion.

As this light of fire kindles easily when it hath been kindled before, so the soul accustomed to the presence of God in holy meditations, though it fall asleep in some dark corner, in some sin of infirmity awhile, yet, upon every holy occasion it takes fire again, and the meanest preacher in the church shall work more upon him than the four doctors of the church should be able to do, upon a person who had never been enlightened before, that is, never accustomed to the presence of God in his private meditations or in his outward acts of religion.

The Light of Precious Stones and the Light of Reflection

In the application of the first of these lights, the light of precious stones, we shall only apply their making and their value. Precious stones are first drops of the dew from heaven, and then refined by the sun of heaven. When by long lying they have exhaled and evaporated and breathed out all their gross matter, and received another concoction from the sun, then they become precious in the eye and estimation of men; so those actions of ours t hat shall be precious or acceptable in the eye of God, must at first have been conceived from heaven, from the Word of God, and then receive another concoction by a holy deliberation, before we bring those actions to execution, lest we may have mistaken the root thereof. Actions precious or acceptable in God's eye must be holy purposes in their beginning and then done in season; the dove must lay the egg and hatch the bird; the Holy Ghost must infuse the purpose and sit upon it and overshadow it and mature and ripen it, if it shall be precious in God's eye.

The reformation of abuses in state or church is a holy purpose, there is that drop of the dew of heaven in it; but if it be unseasonably attempted and have not a farther concoction than the first motions of our own zeal, it becomes ineffectual. Stones precious in the estimation of men begin with the dew of heaven and proceed with the sun of heaven. Actions precious in the acceptation of God are purposes conceived by his Spirit and executed in his time to his glory, not conceived out of ambition nor executed out of sedition. And this is the application of this light of precious stones, out of their making. We proposed another out of their valuation which is this, that whereas a pearl or diamond of such a bigness, of so many carats, is so much worth, one that is twice as big is ten times as much worth. So, though God vouchsafe to value every good work thou dost, yet as they grow greater he shall multiply his estimation of them infinitely. When he hath prized at a high rate the chastity and continency of thy youth, if thou add to this a moderation in thy middle age from ambition, and in thy latter age from covetousness and indevotion, there shall be no price in God's treasure (not the last drop of the blood of his Son) too dear for thee, no room, no state in his kingdom (not a joint tenancy with his only Son) too glorious for thee.

The Light Of Reflection is when God's light cast upon us reflecteth upon other men too, from us; when God doth not only accept our works for ourselves, but employs those works of ours upon other men. And here is a true and a divine supererogation, which the devil (as he doth all God's actions, which fall into his compass) did mischievously counterfeit in the unreformed church when he induced the doctrine of supererogation, that a man might do so much more than he was bound to do for God, as that superplusage might save whom he would; and that if he did not direct them in his intention upon any particular person, the bishop of Rome was general administrator to all men and might bestow them where he would. But here is a true supererogation, not from man or his merit, but from God; when our good works shall not only profit us that do them, but others that see them done; and when we by this light of 'repercussion', of 'reflection,' shall be made looking-glasses as receive God's face upon ourselves and cast it upon others by a holy life and exemplary conversation.

Conclusion

To end all, we have no warmth in ourselves; it is true, but Christ came even in winter. We have no light in ourselves; it is true, but he came even in the night. And now I appeal to your own consciences and I ask you all (not as a judge but as an assistant to your consciences) whether any man have made as good use of this light as he might have done. Is there any man that in the compassing of his sin hath not met this light by the way, 'Thou shouldest not do this'? Any man that hath not only as Balaam did met this light as an angel (that is, met heavenly inspirations to avert him), but that hath not heard as Balaam did, his own ass; that is, those reasons that used to carry him, or those very worldly respects that used to carry him, dispute against that sin and tell him not only that there is more soul and more heaven, and more salvation, but more body and more health, more honour and more reputation, more cost and more money, more labour and more danger spent upon such a sin than would have carried him the right way.

'They that sleep, sleep in the night, and they that are drunk, are drunk in the night'. But to you the day star, the Sun of

Righteousness, the Son of God is risen this day. The day is but a little longer now than at shortest; but a little it is. Be a little better now than when you came, and mend a little at every coming, and in less than seven year's apprenticeage, which your occupations cost you, you shall learn, not the mysteries of your twelve companies, but the mysteries of the twelve tribes, of the twelve apostles, of their twelve articles, whatsoever belongeth to the promise, to the performance, to the imitation of Christ Jesus.

He who is light and light alone, and light and all light, shall also, by that light which he sheddeth from himself upon all his, the light of grace, give you all these attestations, all these witnesses of that his light. He shall give you the light of essence (really and essentially to be incorporated into him, to be made partakers of his divine nature, and the same Spirit with the Lord, by a conversation in heaven, here), and the light of glory (a gladness to give him glory in a denudation of your souls and your sins, by humble confession to him and a gladness to receive a denudation and manifestation of yourselves to yourselves by his messenger, in his medicinal and musical increpations, and a gladness to receive an inchoation of future glory, in the remission of those sins). He shall give you the light of faith (faithful and unremovable possession of future things in the present, and make your hereafter now, in the fruition of God), and the light of nature (a love of the outward beauty of his house and outward testimonies of this love, in inclining your natural faculties to religious duties). He shall give you the light of heavenly bodies (a love to walk in the light of the stars of heaven, that never change, a love so perfect in the fundamental articles of religion, without impertinent additions), and the light of fire (an aptness to take holy fire by what hand, or tongue, or pen soever it be presented unto you, according to God's ordinance, though that light have formerly been suffered to go out in you). He shall give to you the light of precious stones (the lustre of precious stones made of the dew of heaven and by the heat of heaven, that is, actions intended at first, and produced at last, for his glory; and every day multiply their value in the sight of God, because thou shalt every day grow up from grace to grace), and the light of reflection (he shall make you able to reflect and cast this light upon others, to his glory and their establishment).

Lighten our darkness, we beseech thee, O Lord, with all these lights; that in thy light we may see light; that in this essential light, which is Christ, and in this supernatural light, which is grace, we may see all these, and all other beams of light, which may bring us to thee, and him, and that blessed Spirit which proceeds from both.

NOW IN A GLASS, THEN FACE TO FACE

For now we see through a glass darkly, but then face to face; now I know in part, but then I shall know, even as also I am known.

1 Corinthians 13:12

Knowledge

The first act of the will is love, for till the will love, till it would have something, it is not a will. But then . . . it is impossible to love anything till we know it. First our understanding must present it as a known truth, and then our will embraces it as good and worthy to be loved. Therefore Aristotle concludes easily as a thing that admits no contradiction, that naturally all men desire to know that they may love. As St Paul desires to know nothing else, so let no man pretend to know anything but Christ crucified, that is, crucified for him, made his. In the eighth verse of this chapter he says, 'Prophecy shall fail, and tongues shall fail, and knowledge shall vanish', but this knowledge of God in Christ made mine, being crucified for me, shall dwell with me forever.

Sight

First then we consider (before we come to our knowledge of God) our sight of God in this world, and that is, says our Apostle, 'we see as in a glass'. But how do we see in a glass? Truly that is not easily determined. The old writers in the optics said that when we see a thing in a glass we see not the thing itself, but a representation only. All the later men say, we do see the thing itself, but not by direct but by reflected beams. It is a useless labour for the present to reconcile them. This may well consist with both, that as that which we see in a glass assures us that such a thing there is (for we cannot see a dream in a glass, nor a fancy, nor a chimera), so this sight of God, which our Apostle says we have 'in a glass', is enough to assure us that a God there is.

This glass is better than the water; the water gives a crookedness and false dimensions to things that it shows, as we see by an oar when we row a boat. But in the glass which the Apostle intends, we may see God directly, that is, see directly that there is a God. It is a true sight of God, though it be not a perfect sight which we have this way.

The World as a Theatre

Aquinas calls this theatre where we sit and see God, the whole world. And David compasses the world and finds God everywhere, and says at last, 'Whither shall I fly from thy presence? If I ascend up into heaven, thou art there'. At Babel they thought to build to heaven, but did any men ever pretend to get above heaven, above the power of winds, or the impression of other malignant meteors. Can any man get above the power of God? 'If I take wings of the morning, and dwell in the uttermost parts of the sea, there thy right hand shall hold me, and lead me.' If we sail to the waters above the firmament, it is so too. Nay, take a place which God never made, a place which grew out of our sins; that is hell; yet, 'If we make our bed in hell, God is there too'. In a word, whether we be in the Eastern parts of the world, from whom the truth of religion is passed, or in the Western, to which it is not yet come; whether we be in the darkness of ignorance or the darkness of the works of darkness, or darkness of oppression of spirit in sadness, the world is the theatre that represents God, and everywhere every man may, nay must see him.

Every Creature as a Stage

The whole frame of the world is the theatre and every creature the stage, the medium, the glass in which we may see God. There is not so poor a creature but may be thy glass to see God in. The greatest flat glass that can be made cannot represent anything greater than it is. If every gnat that flies were an arch-angel, all that could but tell me, that there is a God, and the poorest worm that creeps tells me that. If I should ask the basilisk how camest thou by those killing eyes, he would tell me, thy God made me so. And if I should ask the slow-worm, how camest thou to be without eyes, he would tell me, thy God made me so. The cedar is no better a glass to see God in than the hysop upon the wall; all things that are, are equally removed from being nothing; and whatsoever hath any being is by that very being a glass in which we see God, who is the root and the fountain of all being. The whole frame of nature is the theatre, the whole volume of creatures is the glass, and the light of reason is our light, which is another circumstance.

The Light of Reason

Of those words (John 1:9), 'That was the true light, that lighteth every man that cometh into the world', the slackest sense that they can admit gives light enough to see God by. If we spare St Chrysostom's sense, that that light is the light of the Gospel and of grace, and that that light considered in itself, and without opposition in us 'does enlighten', that is, would enlighten 'every man', if that man did not wink at that light; if we forbear St Augustine's sense, 'that light enlightens every man', that is, every man that is enlightened is enlightened by that light; if we take but St Cyril's sense, that this light is the light of natural reason which, without question, 'enlightens every man that comes into the world'; yet have we light enough to see God by that light, in the theatre of nature and in the glass of creatures.

God affords no man the comfort, the false comfort of atheism. He will not allow a pretending atheist the power to flatter himself so far as seriously to think there is no God. He must pull out his own eyes and see no creature, before he can say he sees no God. He must be no man and quench his reasonable soul, before he can say to himself, there is no God. The difference between the reason of man and the instinct of the beast is this, that the beast does not know, but the man knows that he knows. The bestial atheist will pretend that he knows there is no God, but he cannot say that he knows that he knows it, for his knowledge will not stand the battery of an argument from another, nor of a ratiocination from himself.

He dares not ask himself, Who is it that I pray to, in a sudden danger, if there be no God? Nay he dares not ask, Who is it that I swear by, in a sudden passion, if there be no God? Whom do I tremble at, and sweat under, at midnight, and whom do I curse by next morning, if there be no God? How weak soever those means which are ordained by God seem to be, and be indeed in themselves, yet they are strong enough to those ends and purposes for which God ordained them.

And so, for such a sight of God as we take the Apostle to intend here, which is to see that there is a God, the frame of nature, the whole world is our theatre, the Book of creatures is our medium, our glass, and natural reason is light enough. But then, for the other degree, the other notification of God, which is the knowing of God, though that also be first to be considered in this world, the means is of a higher nature than served for the sight of God; and yet, whilst we are in this world, it is but an enigma in an obscure riddle, a representation, darkly, and in part, as we translate it.

Knowledge of God

As the glass which we spoke of before, was proposed to the sense, and so we might see God, that is see that there is a God, this enigma that is spoken now, this dark similitude and comparison is proposed to our faith, and so far we know God, that is believe in God in this life, but by enigma, by dark representations and allusions. Therefore says St Augustine, that Moses saw God in that conversation which he had with him in the Mount, removed from all benefit and assistance of bodily senses (he needed not that glass, the help of the creature), and more then so, removed from all allusions, or similitudes, or presentations of God, which might bring God to the understanding and so to the belief. Moses knew God by a more immediate working than either sense, or understanding, or faith. Therefore, by this which the Apostle calls a glass and this which he calls enigma, a dark representation, he understands all things by which God hath notified himself to man: by the glass to his reason, by the enigma to his faith.

The Church as a University

This place where we take our degrees in this knowledge of God, our academy, our university for that, is the Church. For, though, as there may be some few examples given of men that have grown learned who never studied at university, so there may be some examples of men enlightened by God and yet not within that covenant which constitutes the Church, yet the ordinary place for degrees is the university and the ordinary place for illumination in the knowledge of God is the Church. Therefore did God, who ever intended to have his kingdom of heaven well peopled, so powerfully, so miraculously enlarge his way to it, the Church, that it prospered as a wood which no felling, no stubbing, could destroy. We find in the Acts of the Church five thousand martyrs executed in a day, and we find in the Acts of the Apostles five thousand brought to the Church by one sermon; still our Christenings were equal to our burials at least.

Therefore when Christ says to the Church, 'Fear not little flock', it was, says Chrysologus, not because it should fall from great to little, but rise from little to great. Such care had Christ of the growth thereof, and then such care of the establishment and power thereof, as that the first time that ever he names the Church, he invests it with an assurance of perpetuity: 'Upon this Rock will I build my Church, and the gates of hell shall not prevail against it'. Therein is denoted the strength and stability of the Church in itself, and then the power and authority of the Church upon others. For knowledge of God, the Church is our academy; there we must be bred and there we may be bred all our lives and yet learn nothing. Therefore, as we must be there, so there we must use the means, and the means in the Church are the institutions of the Church.

The Institutions of the Church

The most powerful means is the Scripture, but the Scripture in the Church. Not that we are discouraged from reading the Scripture at home: God forbid we should think any Christian family to be out of the Church. At home the Holy Ghost is with thee in the reading of the Scriptures, but there he is with thee as a remembrancer ('The Holy Ghost shall bring to your remembrance whatsoever I have said unto you', says our Saviour). Here in the Church he is with thee as a Doctor to teach thee. First learn at Church and then meditate at home. Receive the seed by hearing the Scriptures interpreted here, and water it by returning to those places at home. When Christ bids you 'Search the Scriptures', he means you should go to them, who have a warrant to search, a warrant in their calling. To know which are Scriptures, to know what the Holy Ghost says in the Scriptures, apply thyself to the Church. Not that the Church is a judge above the Scriptures (for the power and the commission which the Church hath, it hath from the Scriptures), but the Church is a judge above thee, which are the Scriptures and what is the sense of the Holy Ghost in them.

So then thy means are the Scriptures. That is thy evidence. But then this evidence must be sealed to thee in the sacraments and delivered to thee in preaching, and so sealed and delivered to thee in the presence of competent witnesses, the congregation. When St Paul was carried up . . . in an ecstasy 'into Paradise', that which he gained by this powerful way of teaching is not expressed in what he saw, but what he heard. It is not said that he saw, but that he heard unspeakable things. The eye is the devil's door, before the ear, for, though he do enter at the ear by wanton discourse, yet he was at the eye before. We see before we talk dangerously. But the ear is the Holy Ghost's first door. He assists us with ritual and ceremonial things which we see in the Church, but ceremonies have their right use when their right use hath first been taught by preaching. Therefore to hearing does the Apostle apply faith.

The Light of Faith

Those heretics against whom St Chrysostom and others of the fathers writ, were inexcusable in this, that they said they were able to know God in this life as well as God knew himself. But in this more especially lay their impiety, that they said they were able to do all this by the light of nature, without faith. By the light of nature, in the theatre of the world, by the medium of creatures, we see God. But to know God by believing not only Him but in Him is only in the academy of the Church, only through the medium of the institutions there, and only by the light of faith.

The School does ordinarily design four ways of knowing God, and they make the first of these four ways to be by faith; but then by faith they mean no more but an assent that there is a God; which is but that which in our former considerations we called the seeing of God, and which indeed needs not faith; for the light of nature will serve for that, to see God so. They make their second way contemplation, that is an union of God in this life, which is truly the same thing that we mean by faith, for we do not call an assent to the Gospel faith, but faith is the application of the Gospel to ourselves; not an assent that Christ died, but an assurance that Christ died for all. Their third way of knowing God is by apparition, as when God appeared to the patriarchs and others in fire, in angels, or otherwise. And their fourth way is by his clear manifestation of himself in heaven.

Their first way, by assenting only and their third way of apparition, are weak and uncertain ways. The other two, present faith and future vision, are safe ways, but admit this difference, that that of future vision is such a knowledge of God as when it is once had can never be lost nor diminished, but knowledge by faith in this world is an effect and fruit of that grace which God shed upon the whole Communion of Saints, that is, upon all those who in this academy, the Church, do embrace the medium, that is, the institutions of the Church. And this knowledge of God, by this faith, may be diminished and increased, for it is but an enigma says our text, darkly, obscurely; clearly in respect of the natural man but yet obscurely in respect of that knowledge of God which we shall have in heaven; for, says the Apostle, 'As long as we walk by faith, and not by sight, we are absent from the Lord'. Faith is a blessed presence, but compared with heavenly vision it is but an absence, though it create and constitute in us a possibility, a probability, a kind of certainty of salvation, yet that faith, which the best Church hath, is not so far beyond that sight of God which the natural man hath, as that sight of God which I shall have in heaven is above that faith which we have now in the highest exaltation. Therefore there belongs a consideration to that which is added by our Apostle here, that the knowledge which I have of God here (even by faith, through the institutions of the Church) is but a knowledge in part. 'Now I know in part.'

In Part

Though we know by faith, yet for all that faith, it is but a little of a great deal that we know yet, because though faith be good evidence, yet faith is but 'the evidence of things not seen', and there is better evidence of them when they are seen. For, if we consider the object, we cannot believe so much of God, nor of our happiness in him, as we shall see then. For when it is said that the heart comprehends it not, certainly faith comprehends it not neither. And if we consider the manner, faith itself is but darkness in respect of the vision of God in heaven. For those words of the Prophet, 'I will search Jerusalem with candles', are spoken of the times of the Christian Church and of the best men in the Christian Church; yet they shall be searched with candles, some darkness shall be found in them. To the Galatians well instructed and well established, the Apostle says, 'Now after ye have known God, or rather are known of God'. The best knowledge that we have of God here, even by faith, is rather that he knows us, than that we know him. And in this text it is in his own person that the Apostle puts the instance, 'Now I (I, an Apostle, taught by Christ himself) know but in part'. And therefore, as St Augustine saith, 'the love which we bear to our neighbour is but as the infancy, but as the cradle of that love which we bear to God. So that sight of God which we have in the glass', that is in nature, is but the infancy, but the cradle of that knowledge which we have in faith; and yet that knowledge which we have in faith is but the infancy and cradle of that knowledge which we shall have when we come to see God 'face to face'.

Faith is infinitely above nature, infinitely above works, even above those works which faith itself produces, as parents are to children and the tree to the fruit; but yet faith is as much below vision and seeing God face to face. And therefore, though we ascribe willingly to faith more than we can express, yet let no man think himself so infallibly safe, because he finds that he believes in God, as he shall be when he sees God. The faithfulest man in the Church must say, 'Lord increase my faith'. He that is least in the kingdom of heaven shall never be put to that. All the world is but a glass in which we see God. The Church itself and that which the institutions of the Church begets in us, faith itself, is but an enigma, a dark representation of God to us, till we come to that state, 'To see God face to face, and to know, as also we are known'.

The Sphere of Heaven

Now as for the sight of God here, our theatre was the world, our medium and glass was the creature, and our light was reason, and then for our knowledge of God here, our academy was the Church, our medium the institutions of the Church, and our light the light of faith. So we consider the same terms, first for the sight of God and then for the knowledge of God in the next life. First, the sphere, the place where we shall see him is heaven. He that asks me what heaven is means not to hear me, but to silence me; he knows I cannot tell him. When I meet him there, I shall be able to tell him, and then he will be as able to tell me; yet then we shall be but able to tell one another, this, this that we enjoy is heaven, but the tongues of angels, the tongues of glorified saints, shall not be able to express what that heaven is, for even in heaven our faculties shall be finite. Heaven is not a place that was created, for all place that was created shall be dissolved. God did not plant a Paradise for himself and remove to that, as he planted a Paradise for Adam and removed him to that. But God is still where he was before the world was made. And in that place, where there are more suns than there are stars in the firmament (for all the saints are suns), and more light in another sun, the sun of righteousness, the Son of Glory, the Son of God, than in all them in that illustration, that emanation, that effusion of beams of glory, which began not to shine 6,000 years ago, but 6,000 millions of millions before that, in those eternal, in those uncreated heavens, shall we see God.

God's Self-Revelation

This is our sphere and that which we are fain to call our place; and then our medium, our way to see him is God's laying himself open, his manifestation, his revelation, his evisceration, and embowelling of himself to us, there. Doth God never afford this patefaction, this manifestation of himself in his essence to any in this life? We cannot answer yea, nor no, without offending a great part in the School. So many affirm, so many deny, that God hath been seen in his essence in this life. There are that say that it is little less than an article of faith that it has been done; and Aquinas denies it so absolutely as that his followers interpret him, that God by his absolute power cannot make a man, remaining a mortal man, and under the definition of a mortal man, capable of seeing his essence, as we may truly say that God cannot make a beast, remaining in that nature, capable of grace or glory. As it may be fairly argued that Christ suffered not the very torments of hell, because it is essential to the torments of hell to be eternal, they were not torments of hell if they received an end; so it is fairly argued too that neither Adam in his ecstasy in Paradise, nor Moses in his conversation in the Mount, nor the other Apostle in the Transfiguration of Christ, nor St. Paul in his rapture to the third heavens, saw the essence of God, because he that is admitted to that sight of God, can never look off, nor lose that sight again. Only in heaven shall God proceed to this manifestation, this revelation of himself; and that by the light of glory.

The Light of Glory

The light of glory is such a light as that our Schoolmen dare not say confidently that every beam of it is not all of it. When some of them say that some souls see some things in God and others, others, because all have not the same measure of the light of glory, the rest cry down that opinion and say that as the essence of God is indivisible and he that sees any of it sees all of it, so is the light of glory communicated entirely to every blessed soul. God made light first, and three days after that light became a sun, a more glorious light. God gave me the light of nature when I quickened in my mother's womb by receiving a reasonable soul. And God gave me the light of faith when I quickened in my second mother's womb, the Church, by receiving my baptism. But in my third day, when my mortality shall put on immortality, he shall give me the light of glory, by which I shall see himself. To this light of glory the light of honour is but a glow-worm; the majesty itself but a twilight; the cherubims and seraphims are but candles; and that Gospel itself, which the Apostle calls the glorious Gospel, but a star of the least magnitude. And if I cannot tell what to call this light by which I shall see it, what shall I call that which I shall see by it, the essence of God himself? And yet there is something else than this sight of God intended in that which remains. I shall not only 'see God face to face', but I shall 'know' him (which, as you have seen all the way, is above sight) and 'know him, even as also I am known'.

God Alone

In this consideration, God alone is all. In all the former there was a place, and a means, and a light; here, for this perfect knowledge of God, God is all those. 'Then', says the Apostle, 'God shall be all in all'. Says St Jerome, here God does all in all, but here he does all by instruments; even in the infusing of faith he works by the ministry of the Gospel; but there he shall be all in all, do all in all, immediately by himself, for Christ shall deliver up the kingdom to God, even the Father. His kingdom is the administration of his Church by his institutions in the Church. At the resurrection there shall be an end of that kingdom; no more Church; no more working upon men by preaching; but God himself shall be all in all. It may be somewhat too familiarly, too vulgarly said, but usefully, 'The ministry of the Gospel is but as God's vizor', for by such a liberty the Apostle here calls it an enigma, a riddle, or God's picture; but in the resurrection God shall put off that vizor and turn away that picture and show us his own face. Therefore is it said, 'That in heaven there is no temple, but God himself is the temple'. God is service, and music, and psalm, and sermon, and sacrament. 'We shall live upon the word and hear never a word', live upon him, who being the word, was made flesh, the eternal Son of God.

'Here God is not all in all; where he is at all in any man, that man is well.' It was well with Solomon, because God was wisdom with him, and patience in Job, and faith in Peter, and zeal in Paul; but there was something in all these, which God was not. But in heaven he shall be so all in all that every soul shall have every perfection in itself; and the perfection of these perfections shall be that their sight shall be 'face to face', and their knowledge 'as they are known'.

Face to Face

Since St Augustine calls it a debt, a double debt, a debt because she asked it, a debt because he promised it, to give even a woman, Paulina, satisfaction in that high point and mystery, 'how we should see God face to face in heaven', it cannot be unfit in this congregation to ask and answer some short questions concerning that. Is it always a declaration of favour when God shows his face? No. 'I will set my face against that soul, that eateth blood, and cut him off.' But when there is light joined with it, it is a declaration of favour. This was the blessing that God taught Moses for Aaron, to bless the people with, 'The Lord make his face to shine upon thee, and be gracious to thee.' And there we shall 'see him face to face', by the light of his countenance, which is the light of glory. What shall we see, by seeing him so, 'face to face'? We shall see whatsoever we can be the better for seeing. First of all, all things that they believed here, they shall see there; and therefore let us meditate upon no other things on earth than we would be glad to think on in heaven. And this consideration would put many frivolous and many fond thoughts out of our mind, if men and women would love another but so, as that love might last in heaven.

This then we shall get concerning ourselves, by seeing God 'face to face', but what concerning God? Nothing but the sight of the humanity of Christ, which only is visible to the eye. So Theodoret, so some others have thought, but that answers not. And we know we shall see God (not only the body of Christ) as he is in his essence. Why? Did all that are said 'to have seen God face to face' see his essence? No. In earth God assumed some material things to appear in and is said 'to have been seen face to face' when he was seen in those assumed forms. But in heaven there is no material thing to be assumed, and if God be seen face to face there, he is seen in his essence. St Augustine sums it up fully, upon these words, 'In thy light we shall see light, we shall see thee in thee'; that is, says he, 'face to face'.

In Order to Know

And then, what is it 'to know him, as we are known'? First, is that it which is intended here, 'That we shall know God as we are known'? It is not expressed in the text so. It is only 'that we shall know so', not 'that we shall know God so'. But the frame and context of the place hath drawn that unanimous exposition from all that it is meant of our knowledge of God then. A comprehensive knowledge of God it cannot be. To comprehend is to know a thing as well as that thing can be known; and we can never know God, so, but that he will know himself better. Our knowledge cannot be so dilated, nor God condensed and contracted so, as that we can know him that way, comprehensively. It cannot be such a knowledge of God as God hath of himself, nor as God hath of us; for God comprehends us and all this world and all the worlds that he could have made, and himself. But it is not equal, but similar. As God knows me, so I shall know God; but I shall not know God so as God knows me. It is not as much, but as truly; as the fire does as truly shine as the sun shines, though it shine not out so far, nor to so many purposes. So then I shall know God so as that there shall be nothing in me to hinder me from knowing God; which cannot be said of the nature of man, though regenerate, upon earth, no, nor of the nature of an angel in heaven, left to itself, till both have received a super-illustration from the light of glory.

And so it shall be a knowledge so like his knowledge, as it shall produce a love like his love, and we shall love him as he loves us. For, as St Chrysostom and the rest of the fathers interpret it, 'I shall know him, that is embrace him, adhere to him'. What a Holy-day shall this be, which no working day shall ever follow! By knowing and loving the unchangeable, the immutable God, we shall be changed into an unchangeableness, says that father that never said anything but extraordinarily. He says more, 'If God could be seen and known in hell, hell in an instant would be heaven'.

How many heavens are there in heaven? How is heaven multiplied to every soul in heaven, where infinite other happinesses are crowned with this, this sight and this knowledge of God there? And how shall all those heavens be renewed to us every day, that shall be as glad to see and to know God, millions of ages after every day's seeing and knowing, as the first hour of looking upon his face. And as this seeing and this knowing of God crowns all other joys and glories, even in heaven, so this very crown is crowned. There grows from this a higher glory, which is 'imperishable and undefiled', (words of which Luther says, that both testaments afford none equal to them), 'that we shall be made partakers of the Divine nature' – immortal as the Father, righteous as the Son, and full of all comfort as the Holy Ghost.

Let me dismiss you with an easy request of St Augustine, 'that man does not love God, that loves not himself'. Do but love yourselves.

'Only that man that loves God, hath the art of love to himself.' Do but love yourselves. For if he love God, he would live eternally with him, and if he desire that, and endeavour it earnestly, he does truly love himself, and not otherwise. And he loves himself, who by seeing God in the theatre of the world, and in the glass of the creature, by the light of reason, and knowing God in the academy of the Church, by the institution thereof, through the light of faith, endeavours to see God in heaven, by the manifestation of himself, through the light of glory, and to know God himself, in himself, and by himself as he is all in all; contemplatively by knowing as he is known, practically by loving as he is loved.

PRAYER AND THE DIVINE MERCY

Father, forgive them, for they know not what they do.
Luke 23:34

The Word Of God

The word of God is either the co-eternal and co-essential Son, our Saviour, which took flesh, or it is the spirit of his mouth, by which we live, and not by bread only. And so, in a large acceptation, every truth is the Word of God; for truth is uniform, and irrepugnant, and indivisible, as God.

More strictly the Word of God is that which God has uttered, either in writing, as twice in the Tablets to Moses; or by ministry of angels, or prophets, in words; or by the unborn, in action, as in John the Baptist's exultation within his mother; or by new-born, from the mouths of babes and sucklings, or by things unreasonable, as in Balaam's ass; or insensible, as in the whole book of such creatures, 'The heavens declare the glory of God'. But nothing is more properly the Word of God to us than that which God himself speaks in those organs and instruments which himself has assumed for his chief work, our redemption. For in creation God spoke, but in redemption he did; and more, he suffered. And of that kind are these words. God in his chosen manhood says, 'Father forgive them, for they know not what they do'.

These words shall be fitliest considered, like a goodly palace, if we rest a little, as in an outward court, upon consideration of prayer in general; and then draw near the view of the palace, in a second court, considering this special prayer in general as the face of the whole palace. Thirdly, we will pass through the chief rooms of the palace itself; and then insist upon four steps: 1. Of whom he begs (Father). 2. What he asks (forgive them). 3. That he prays upon reason (for). 4. What the reason is (they know not).

Of Prayer

So therefore prayer is our first entry, for when it is said, 'Ask and it shall be given', it is also said, 'Knock and it shall be opened', showing that by prayer our entrance is. And not the entry only, but the whole house: 'My house is the house of prayer.' Of all the conduits and conveyances of God's graces to us, none has been so little subject to cavillations as this of prayer. The sacraments have fallen into the hands of flatterers and robbers. Some have attributed too much to them, some detracted. Some have painted them, some have withdrawn their natural complexion. It has been disputed whether they be, how many they be, what they be, and what they do. The preaching of the Word has been made a servant of ambitions and a shop of many men's new-fangled wares. Almost every means between God and man suffers some adulteratings and disguises, but prayer least; and it has most ways and addresses. It may be mental, for we may think prayers. It may be vocal, for we may speak prayers. It may be actual, for we do prayers. For deeds have voice, the vices of Sodom did cry, and the alms of Tobit. And if it were proper for St John in the first of the Revelations to turn back and to see a voice, it is more likely God will look down to hear a work. So then to do the office of your vocation sincerely is to pray. How much the favourites of princes and great personages labour that they may be thought to have been in private conference with the prince. And though they be forced to wait upon his purposes, and talk of what he will, how fain they would be thought to have solicited their own, or their dependent's business. With the Prince of Princes, this every man may do truly; and the sooner, the more beggar he is, for no man is heard here but as a beggar.

Here we may talk long, welcomely, of our own affairs, and be sure to speed. You cannot whisper so low alone in your chamber but he hears you, nor sing so loud in the congregation but he distinguishes you. He grudges not to be chidden and disputed with, by Job. 'The arrows of the Almighty are in me, and the venom thereof hath drunk up my spirit. Is my strength the strength of stones, or is my flesh of brass?' Not to be directed and counselled by Jonah, who was angry and said, 'Did not I say, when I was in my country, thou wouldest deal thus?' And when the Lord said, 'Doest thou well to be angry?' he replies, 'I do well to be angry to the death.' Nor almost to be threatened and neglected by Moses: 'Do this, or blot my name out of thy book.' It is an honour to be able to say to servants, 'Do this': but to say to God, 'Lord, do this,' and prevail, is more; and yet more easy.

God is replenishingly everywhere; but most contractedly and workingly in the temple. Since then every rectified man is the temple of the Holy Ghost, when he prays; it is the Holy Ghost itself that prays. And what can be denied where the asker gives? He plays with us, as children, shows us pleasing things, that we may cry for them, and have them. 'Before we call, he answers; and when we speak, he hears:' says Isaiah. Physicians observe some symptoms so violent that they must neglect the disease for a time and labour to cure the accident; as burning fevers, in dysenteries. So in the sinful consumption of the soul, a stupidity and indisposition to prayer must first be cured. For 'Ye lust, and have not, because ye ask not,' says Isaiah. The adulterous mother of the three great brothers, Gratian, Lombard, and Comestor, being warned by her confessor to be sorry for her act, said she could not, because her fault had so much profited the Church. 'At least', said he, 'be sorry that you cannot be sorry.' So whosoever you be, that cannot readily pray, at least pray that you may pray. For, as in bodily, so in spiritual diseases, it is a desperate state to be speechless.

Father

It were unmannerliness to hold you longer in the entry. One turn in the inner court, of this special prayer in general, and so enter the palace. This is not a prayer for his own ease, as that in his agony seems. It has none of those infirmities which curious schismatics find in that. No suspicion of ignorance, as there ('if it be possible'). No tergiversation nor abandoning the noble work which he had begun, as there ('let this cup pass'). It is not an exemplar, or form, for us to imitate precisely (otherwise than in the doctrine), as that prayer which we call the Lord's Prayer, not because he said it, for he could never say 'forgive us our trespasses', but because he commanded us to say it. For though by Matthew, which says, 'After this manner pray', we seem not bound to the words, yet Luke says, 'When you pray, say, Our Father which art, etc.' But this is a prayer of God, to God; . . . as when foreign merchandise is misported, the prince may permit or inhibit his subjects to buy it, or not to buy it. Our blessed Saviour arriving in this world freighted with salvation, a thing which this world never had power to have without him, except in that short time between man's creation and fall, he by this prayer begs that even to these despisers of it, it may be communicable, and that their ignorance of the value of it may not deprive them of it. Teaching that by example here, which he gave in precept before, 'Pray for them which persecute you, that you may be the children of your Father which is in heaven'. Therefore, doing so now, he might well say, 'Father, forgive them', which is the first room in this glorious palace.

And in this contemplation, O my unworthy soul, you are presently in the presence. No passing of guards, nor ushers. No examination of your degree or habit. The prince is not asleep, nor private, nor weary of giving, nor refers to others. He puts you not to prevail by angels nor archangels. But lest anything might hinder you from coming into his presence, his presence comes into you. And lest majesty should dazzle you, you are to speak but to your Father. Of which word, *Abba*, the root is 'to will'; from which root, the fruit also must be willingness and propenseness to grant. God is the Father of Christ, by that mystical and eternal inexpressible generation, which never began nor ended. Of which incomprehensible mystery, Moses and the ancient prophets spake so little, and so indirectly, that till the dawning of the day of Christ, after Esdras' time, those places seem not to be intended of the Trinity. Nay, a good while after Christ they were but tenderly applied to that sense. And at this day, the most of the writers in the reformed Churches, considering that we need not such far-fetched and such forced helps, and withal weighing how well the Jews of these times are provided with other expositions of those places, are very sparing in using them, but content themselves modestly herein with the testimonies of the New Testament.

Truly, this mystery is rather the object of faith than reason; and it is enough that we believe Christ to have ever been the Son of God, by such generation, and ourselves his sons by adoption. So that God is Father to all; but yet so, that though Christ say, 'My Father is greater than all', he adds, 'I and my Father are all one', to show his eternal interest; and he seems to put a difference 'I go to my Father, and your Father, my God and your God'. The Roman stories have that when Claudius saw it conduce to his ends to get the tribuneship, of which he was incapable because a patrician, he suffered himself to be adopted. But against this adoption two exceptions were found: one, that he was adopted by a man of lower rank, a plebeian, which was unnatural; and by a younger man than himself, which took away the presentation of a father. But our adoption is regular. For first, we are made the sons of the Most High, and thus also by the Ancient of Days. There was no one word, by which he could so nobly have maintained his dignity, kept his station, justified his cause, and withal expressed his humility and charity, as this, 'Father'. They crucified him for saying himself to be the Son of God. And in the midst of torments, he both professes the same still, and lets them see that they have no other way of forgiveness, but that he is the Son of that Father, 'For no man cometh to the Father but by the Son'.

Forgive Them

And at this voice (Father) O most blessed Saviour, your Father, which is so fully yours that for your sake he is ours too; which is so wholly yours that he is yourself; which is all mercy, yet will not spare you; all justice, yet will not destroy us. And that glorious army of Angels, which hitherto by their own integrity maintained their first and pure condition, and by this work of yours, now near the consummation, attend a confirmation and infallibility of ever remaining so. And that faithful company of departed saints, to whom your merit must open a more inward and familiar room in your Father's Kingdom, stand all attentive to hear what you will ask of this Father. And what shall they hear? What do you ask? 'Forgive them', forgive them? Must murderers be forgiven? Must the offended ask it? And must a Father grant it? And must he be solicited and remembered by the name of Father to do it? Was not your passion enough, but you must have compassion? And is your mercy so violent, that you will have a fellow feeling of their imminent afflictions, before they have any feeling? The Angels might expect a present employment for their destruction: the Saints might be out of fear, that they should be assumed or mingled in their fellowship. But you will have them pardoned. And yet dost not out of your own fulness pardon them, as you did the thief upon the cross, because he did already confess you; but you tell them, that they may be forgiven but at your request, and if they acknowledge their advocate to be the Son of God. 'Father, forgive them.'

I that cannot revenge your quarrel cannot forgive them. I that could not be saved, but by their offence, cannot forgive them. And must a Father, Almighty, and well pleased in you, forgive them? You are more charitable towards them, than by your direction we may be to ourselves. We must pray for ourselves limitedly: forgive us, as we forgive. But you will have their forgiveness illimited and unconditioned. You seem not so much as to presume a repentance; which is so essential and necessary in all transgressions, as where by man's fault the actions of God are diverted from his appointed ends, God himself is content to repent the doing of them. As he repented first the making of man, and then the making of a king. But God will have them within the arms of his general pardon. And we are all delivered from our debts, for God has given his word, his co-essential word, for us all. And though (as in other prodigal debts, the interest exceed the principal) our actual sins exceed our original, yet God by giving his word for us has acquitted all.

For

But the affections of our Saviour are not inordinate, nor irregular. He has a 'for' for his prayer: 'Forgive them, for, etc.' And where he has not this 'for', as in his prayer in his agony, he quickly interrupts the violence of his request, with a but, 'Father, let this cup pass, but not my will.' In that form of prayer which himself taught us, he has appointed a 'for', on God's part, which is ever the same unchangeable: 'For thine is the kingdom.' Therefore supplications belong to you: the power, 'Thou openest thy hand and fillest every living thing'; the glory, 'for thy Name is glorified in thy grants.' But because on our part the occasions are variable, he has left our 'for' to our religious discretion. For when it is said, 'You lust and have not, because you ask not', it follows presently, 'You ask and miss, because you ask amiss.' It is not a fit 'for,' for every private man to ask much means for he would do much good. I must not pray, Lord put into my hands the strength of Christian Kings, for out of my zeal I will employ your benefits to your advantage, your soldiers against your enemies, and be a bank against that deluge wherewith your enemy the Turk threatens to overflow your people. I must not pray, 'Lord fill my heart with knowledge and understanding', for I would compose the schisms in your Church, and reduce your garment to the first continual and seamless integrity; and redress the deafnesses and oppressions of judges, and officers. But he gave us a convenient scantling for our 'fors,' who prayed, 'Give me enough, for I may else despair, give me not too much, for so I may presume.'

Of Schoolmen, some affirm prayer to be an act of our will; for we would have that which we ask. Others, of our understanding; for by it we ascend to God, and better our knowledge, which is the proper aliment and food of our understanding; so that is a perplexed case. But all agree that it is an act of our reason, and therefore must be reasonable. For only reasonable things can pray; for the beasts and ravens are not said to pray for food, but 'to cry'.

They Know Not

Let us now (not in curiosity but for instruction) consider the reason: 'They know not what they do.' First, if ignorance excuse and then, if they were ignorant.

Have you, O God, filled all your Scriptures, both of your recorders and notaries, which have penned the history of your love to your people; and of your secretaries the prophets, admitted to the foreknowledge of your purposes, and instructed in your cabinet; have you filled these with phrases and persuasions of wisdom and knowledge, and must these persecutors be pardoned for their ignorance? Have you bid Isaiah to say,

'It is a people of no understanding, therefore he that made them, shall not have compassion of them.' And Hosea 'My people are destroyed for lack of knowledge'; and now do you say, 'Forgive them because they know not?' Shall ignorance, which is often the cause of sin, often a sin itself, often the punishment of sin, and ever an infirmity and disease contracted by the first great sin, advantage them? 'Who can understand his faults?' said the man according to your heart, 'Lord cleanse me from my secret faults.' He durst not make his ignorance the reason of his prayer, but prayed against ignorance.

But your mercy is as the sea: both before it was the sea, for it overspreads the whole world; and since it was called into limits, for it is not the less infinite for that. And as by the sea the most remote and distant nations enjoy one another by traffic and commerce, East and West becoming neighbours, so by mercy the most different things are united and reconciled: sinners have heaven; traitors are in the prince's bosom; and ignorant persons are in the spring of wisdom, being forgiven, not only though they be ignorant, but because they are ignorant. But all ignorance is not excusable; nor any less excusable than not to know what ignorance is not to be excused. Therefore, there is an ignorance which is not knowing of things not appertaining to us. This we had had, though Adam had stood; and the angels have it, for they know not the latter day, and therefore for this we are not chargeable. They call the other privation, which if it proceed merely from our own sluggishness, in not searching the means made for our instruction, is ever inexcusable. If from God, who for his own just ends has cast clouds over those lights which should guide us, it is often excusable. For Paul says, 'I was a blasphemer, and a persecutor, and an oppressor, but I was received to mercy, for I did it ignorantly, through unbelief.' So though we are all bound to believe, and therefore faults done by unbelief cannot escape the name and nature of sin, yet since belief is the immediate gift of God, faults done by unbelief, without malicious concurrences and circumstances, obtain mercy and pardon from that abundant fountain of grace, Christ Jesus.

And therefore it was a just reason, 'Forgive them, for they know not.' If they knew not, which is evident both by this speech from truth itself, and by the verse 'Had they known it, they would not have crucified the Lord of glory'; and the verse 'I know that through ignorance ye did it.' And though after so many powerful miracles, this ignorance were vincible, God having revealed enough to convert them, yet there seems to be enough on their parts to make it a perplexed case, and to excuse, though not a malicious persecuting, yet a not consenting to his doctrine. For they had a law, 'Whosoever shall make himself the son of God, let him die.' And they spoke out of their laws, when they said, 'We have no other King but Caesar.' There were therefore some among them reasonable and zealously ignorant. And for those, the Son ever-welcome and well heard, begged of his Father, ever accessible and exorable, a pardon ever ready and natural.

I acknowledged my sin unto thee, and mine iniquity have I not hid. I said, I will confess my transgressions unto the Lord, and thou forgavest the iniquity of my sin.
Psalm 32:5

Confession

True confession is a mysterious art. As there is a 'mystery of iniquity', so there is a 'mystery of the Kingdom of Heaven'. And the mystery of the Kingdom of Heaven is this, that no man comes thither, but in a sort as he is a notorious sinner. One mystery of iniquity is that in this world, though I multiply sins, yet the judge cannot punish me if I can hide them from other men, though he know them. But if I confess them he can, he will, he must. The mystery of the Kingdom of Heaven is that only the declaring, the publishing, the notifying, and confessing of my sins possesses me of the Kingdom of Heaven. There is a case in which the notoriety of my sin, by way of glory in that sin, casts a scandal upon others and leads them into tentation; for so my sin becomes theirs because they sin my sin by example. And their sin becomes mine because I gave the example, and we aggravate one another's sin, and both sin both. But there is a publication of sin that both alleviates, nay annihilates my sin, and makes him that hates sin, Almighty God, love me the better for knowing me to be such a sinner, than if I had not told him of it. Therefore do we speak of the mystery of confession; for it is not delivered in one rule, nor practised in one act.

In this confession of David's ('I acknowledged my sin unto thee', etc.) we shall see more than so; for, though our two parts be but the two acts, David's act and God's act, confession and absolution, yet is there more than one single action to be considered in each of them. For first, in the first, there is a reflected act, that David doth upon himself before he come to his confession to God; something David had done before he came to say, 'I will confess', as he did 'confess', before God 'forgave the iniquity of his sin'. Now that which he did in himself, and which preceded his confession to God, was the 'I acknowledged my sins'; which was not his bringing it to the knowledge of God by way of confession. For (as you see by the method of the Holy Ghost in the frame of the text) it preceded his purpose of confessing, but it was the taking knowledge of his sin in himself. It was his first quickening and animation, that grace gave his soul, as the soul gives the child in the mother's womb. And then in David's act upon himself, follows the 'I have not hid mine iniquity', none of mine iniquities from mine own sight. I have displayed to myself, anatomized mine own conscience, left no corner unsearched, I am come to a perfect understanding of mine own case. This is David's act upon himself, the recalling and recollecting of his sins, in his own memory. And then finding the number, the weight, and so the oppression of those sins there, he considers where he may discharge himself of them. And 'I will speak' says David, which is a word that implies both deliberation and resolution, and execution, too, I thought what was best to do and I resolved upon this and did it. I will make a true, a full, a hearty confession to God of all those sins; for such we see the elements and the extent of his confession to be. He will confess 'peccata', transgressions, sins; neither by an overtenderness, and diffidence, and scrupulosity to call things sins that are not sin nor by indulgent flattering and sparing of himself to forbear those things which are truly so. He will confess 'sins', and 'his sins'. He will acknowledge them to have proceeded, and to have been committed by himself, he will not impute them to any other cause, least of all to God. And then he will confess sins that are his own sins and not meddle with the sins of other men, that appertain not to him.

This is the subject of his confession, 'sins', and 'his sins', and then 'His sins unto the Lord', both in that consideration, that all sins are committed against the Lord, and in that also, that confession of all sins is to be made unto the Lord. And lastly, all this (as

St Jerome reads this text, and so also did our former translation) 'against himself', that is, without any hope of relief or reparation in himself. He begins to think of his own sinful state and he proceeds to a particular inquisition upon his conscience; there is his preparation. Then he considers and thereupon resolves, and thereupon proceeds to confess things that are truly sins. And then all them as his own, without imputing them to others, if they be his own, without meddling with others, and these to the Lord against whom all sin is committed, and to whom all confession is to be directed. And all this still against himself, without any hope from himself. All this is in David's action, preparatorily in himself and then declaratorily towards God, and do but make up our first part.

In the other, which is God's act towards David, the absolution, the remission, the forgiveness, we shall consider first the fulness. For it is both of the sin and the punishment of the sin, for the word imports both. And then we shall consider the seasonableness, the speed, the acceleration of God's mercy in the absolution. David did but say, I will confess and God forgave the iniquity and the punishment of his sin. Now as this distribution is paraphrase enough upon the text, so a little larger paraphrase upon every piece of paraphrase will be as much as will fall into this exercise. For, as you see, the branches are many and full of fruit, and I can but shake them and leave every one to gather his own portion, to apply those notes which may most advance his edification.

I Acknowledge My Sins

First then in this mystery of confession, we consider David's reflected act, his preparatory act, preceding his confession to God and transacted in himself, of which the first motion is the acknowledgement. I acknowledged in myself, I came to a feeling in myself what my sinful condition was. This is our quickening in our regeneration and second birth. And till this come a sinner lies as the chaos in the beginning of the creation, before the 'Spirit of God had moved upon the face of the waters, dark', and 'void', and 'without form'. He lies, as we may conceive, out of the authors of natural story, the slime and mud of the river Nilus to lie, before the sunbeams strike upon it; which after, by the heat of those beams, produces several shapes and forms of creatures. So till this first beam of grace, which we consider here, strike upon the soul of a sinner, he lies in the mud and slime, in the dregs and lees and tartar of his sin. He cannot as much as wish that that sun would shine upon him. He does not so much as know that there is such a sun that has that influence and impression. But if this first beam of grace enlighten him to himself, reflect upon himself, if it acquaint him with himself, then, as the creatures in the creation, then, as the new creatures at Nilus, his sins begin to take their forms, and their specifications, and they appear to him in their particular true shapes, and that which he hath in a general name called pleasure or wantonness now calls itself in his conscience a direct adultery, a direct incest. And that which he hath called frugality and providence for family and posterity, tells him plainly, my name is oppression and I am the spirit of covetousness.

God by his ordinance, executed by us, brings him to this acknowledgement into company with himself, unto an acquaintance and conversation with himself, and he sees his sins look with other faces, and he hears his sins speak with other voices, and he finds them to call one another by other names. And when he is thus come to that consideration, Lord! How I have mistaken myself. Am I that thought myself and passed with others for a sociable, a pleasurable man, and good company; am I a leprous adulterer; is that my name? Am I that thought myself a frugal man and a good husband, I whom fathers would recommend to their children and say, mark how he spares, how he grows up, how he gathers; am I an oppressing extortioner; is that my name?

Blessed be thy name, O Lord, that hast brought me to this acknowledgement to know mine own name, mine own miserable condition. He will also say, may that blessing of thine enlarge itself father, that as I am come to this acknowledgement, to know that I mistook myself all this while, so I may proceed to the perfect sifting of my conscience, in all corners: which is David's second motion in his act of preparation, and our next consideration, 'I acknowledged my sin', and I hid none, disguised none.

I Hide None

Sometimes the magistrate is informed of an abuse and yet proceeds to no farther search nor inquisition. This word implies a sifting of the conscience. He doth not only take knowledge of his sins than when they discover themselves; of his riot and voluptuousness than when he burns in a fever occasioned by his surfeits; nor of his licentiousness than when he is under the anguish and smart of corrosives; nor of his wastefulness and pride than when he is laid in prison for debt: He doth not seek his sins in his belly nor in his bones, nor in his purse, but in his conscience, and he unfolds that, rips up that, and enters into the privatest and most remote corners thereof. And there is much more in this negative circumstance, I hid nothing, than in the former acknowledgement, I took knowledge of my sins.

But any thing serves for a cover of sin, even from a net, that every man sees through, to such a cloud of darkness as none but the prince of darkness, that cast that cloud upon us, can see us in it, nor we see ourselves. That we should hide lesser sins with greater is not strange; that in an adultery we should forget the circumstances in it and the practices to come to it. But we hide greater sins with lesser, with a manifold and multiplied throng and cloud of lesser sins. Easiness of conversation with a woman seems no great harm. Adorning themselves to please those with whom they converse, is not much more. To hear them whom they are thus willing to please, praise them and magnify their perfections, is little more than that. To allow them to sue and solicit for possession of that which they have so much praised, is not much more neither. Nor will it seem much at last, to give them possession of that they sue for; nay it will seem a kind of injustice to deny it them. We hide lesser sins with greater, greater with lesser. Nay we hide the devil with God, we hide all the week's sins with a sabbath's solemnity: and this is a possession of God, a making the devil to enter into God, when we hide our sins with an outward sanctity and call God to witness and testify to the congregation that we are saints, when we are devils; for this is a subborning of God, and a drawing of God himself into a perjury.

I Speak

This word, 'speak', is a word that implies first meditation, deliberation, considering, and then upon such meditation, a resolution too, and execution after all. When it is said of God, God said this and said that in the first creation, do not think that God uttered a sound; his speaking was inward, his speaking was thinking. So David uses this word in the person of another, 'the fool hath spoken', that is, 'in his heart', that is, thought 'that there is no God'. There speaking is thinking; and speaking is resolving too. So David's son Solomon uses the word, 'Behold I purpose to build a house unto the Lord', where the word is 'I say', I will do it, speaking is determining; and speaking is executing too, 'I said I will take heed to my ways', that is, I will proceed and go forward in the paths of God. And such a premeditation, such a preconsideration, do all our approaches and accesses to God, and all our acts in his service require.

God is the rock of our salvation. God is no occasional God, no accidental God; neither will God be served by occasion, nor by accident, but by a constant devotion. Our communication with God must not be in interjections that come in by chance, nor our devotions made up of parentheses that might be left out. They err equally that make a god of necessity and that make a god of contingency; they that with the Manichees make an ill god, a god that forces men to do all the ill that they do, and they that with the Epicures make an idle god, an indifferent god, that cares not what is done. God is not destiny; then there could be no reward or punishment; but God is not fortune neither, for then there were no providence. If God have given reason only to man, it were strange that man should exercise that reason in all his moral and civil actions and only do the acts of God's worship casually. Not to consider the nature of confession and absolution, not to consider the nature of the sins we should confess and be absolved of, is a stupidity against David's practice here. He spoke, he meditated, he considered God's service is no extemporal thing. But then he resolved too, for so the word signifies, consideration, but resolution upon it; and then, that he resolved, he executed.

I Confess

It is but a homely metaphor, but it is a wholesome and a useful one, confession works as a vomit. It shakes the frame and it breaks the bed of sin, and it is an ease to the spiritual stomach, to the conscience, to be thereby disburdened. It is an ease to the sinner, to the patient; but that that makes it absolutely necessary is that it is a glory to God; for in all my spiritual actions, appreciations or depreciations, whether I pray for benefits or against calamities, still my Alpha and Omega, my first and last motive, must be the glory of God. Therefore Joshua says to Achan, 'My son, give I pray thee, glory unto the Lord God of Israel, and make confession unto him.' Now, the glory of God arises not out of the confessing, but because every true confessing is accompanied with a detestation of the sin, as it hath separated me from God, and a sense of my reunion and redintegration with God, in the abjuration of my former sins (for to tell my sin by way of a good tale, or by boasting in it, though it be a revealing, a manifesting, it is not a confession). In every true confessing God hath glory, because he hath a strayed soul reunited to his kingdom. And to advance this glory, David confesses his sins, which is our next consideration, 'I said, I will confess my sins unto the Lord.'

True Sins

First, he resents his state, all is not well. Then he examines himself, thus and thus it stands with me. Then he considers, then he resolves, then he executes, he confesses (so far are we gone), and now he confesses sins. For the Pharisee's (though he pretended a confession) was rather an exprobation, how much God had been beholden to him, for his sabbaths, for his alms, for his tithes, for his fasting. David confesses sins; first, such things as were truly sins. For as the element of air that lies between the water and the fire is sometimes condensed into water, sometimes rarified into fire; so lies the conscience of man between two operations of the devil. Sometimes he rarifies it, evaporates it, that is apprehends nothing, feels nothing to be sin; sometimes he condenses it, that everything falls and sticks upon it, in the nature, and takes the weight of sin, and he misinterprets the indifferent actions of others, and of his own, and destroys all Christian liberty, all conversation, all recreation, and out of a false fear of being undutiful to God is unjust to all the world and to his own soul, and consequently to God himself, who of all notions would not be received in the notion of a cruel or tyrannical God.

In an obdurate conscience that feels no sin, the devil glories most, but in the over-tender conscience he practices most. This is his triumphant, but this is his militant church. That is his sabbath, but this is his six days labour. In the obdurate he hath induced a security, in the scrupulous and over-tender he is working for desperation. There are few things in the Scriptures which the Holy Ghost hath expressed in so many names as sin: 'sin, wickedness, iniquity, transgressions, offences', many, many more. And all this, that thereby we might reflect upon ourselves often, and see if our particular actions fell not under some of those names. But then, lest this should over-intimidate us, there are as many names given by the Holy Ghost to the Law of God: 'Law, Statutes, Ordinances, Covenants, Testimony, Precept', and all the rest, of which there is some one at least repeated in every verse of the hundred and nineteenth psalm; that thereby we might still have a rule to measure and try our actions by, whether they be sins or no. For, as the Apostle says, 'He had not known sin if he had not known the Law.' So there had been no sin if there had been no Law. And therefore that soul that feels itself oppressed under the burden of a vow, must have recourse to the Law of God, and see whether that vow fall under the rule of that Law. For as an over-tender conscience may call things sins that are not, and so be afraid of things that never were, so may it also of things that were but are not now; of such sins as were truly sins and fearful sins but are now dead, dead by a true repentance and buried in the sea of the blood of Christ Jesus, and sealed up in that monument, under the seal of reconciliation, the blessed sacrament, and yet rise sometimes in this tender conscience, in a suspicion and jealousie, that God hath not truly, not fully forgiven them.

And as a ghost, which we think we see, affrights us more than an army that we do see; so these apparitions of sins, of things that are not against any Law of God, and so are not sins, or sins that are dead in a true repentance, and so have no being at all, by the devil's practice work dangerously upon a distempered conscience. For as God hath given the soul an imagination, and a fancy, as well as an understanding, so the devil imprints in the conscience a false imagination, as well as a fearful sense of true sin. David confesses sins, sins that are truly sins.

All Sins

But the more ordinary danger is in our not calling those things which are truly sins by that name. For, as sometimes when the baptism of a child is deferred for state, the child dies unbaptized: so the sinner defers the baptism of his sin, in his tears and in the blood of the Saviour offered in the blessed sacrament, till he die nameless, nameless in the Book of Life. It is a character that one of the ancientest of poets gives of a well-bred and well-versed gentleman, that he would not tell such lies as were like truths, not probable lies; nor such truths as were like lies, not wonderful, not incredible truths. It is the constancy of a rectified Christian not to call his indifferent actions sins, for that is to slander God, as a cruel God; nor to call sins indifferent actions, for that is to undervalue God, as a negligent God. God doth not keep the conscience of man upon the wrack, in a continual torture and stretching; but God doth not stupefy the conscience with an opiate in an insensibleness of any sin. The Law of God is the balance and the criterion. By that try thine actions, and then confess. David did so. He confessed sins;

nothing that was not so as such; neither omitted he anything that was so. And then they were, 'his sins'; 'I said, I will confess my sins unto the Lord.'

Forgiveness

This is a wide door, and would let out armies of instructions to you; but we will shut up this door, with these two leaves thereof: the fulness of God's mercy, 'He forgives the sin and the punishment'; and the seasonableness, the acceleration of his mercy in this expression of our text. David says 'I will confess' and he knows that God has already forgiven the iniquity. These will be the two leaves of this door. And let the hand that shuts them be this 'and', this particle of connection which we have in the text, 'I said, and thou didst'. For though this remission of sin be not presented here as an effect upon that cause of David's confession, yet it is at least as a consequent from an occasion, so assured, so infallible, as let any man confess as David did, and he shall be sure to be forgiven as David was. For though this forgiveness be a flower of mercy, yet the root grows in the justice of God. If we acknowledge our sin, he is faithful and just to forgive us our sin. It grows out of his faithfulness, as he hath vouchsafed to bind himself by a promise, and out of his justice, as he hath received a full satisfaction for all our sins. So that this hand, this 'and', in our text, is as a ligament, as a sinew, to connect and knit together that glorious body of God's preventing grace and his subsequent grace. If our confession come between and tie the knot, God that moved us to that act will perfect all.

Fulness

Here enters the fulness of his mercy, at one leaf of this door; well expressed at our door in that 'Behold, I stand at the door and knock' for first he comes; here is no mention of our calling of him before; he comes of himself; and then he suffers not us to be ignorant of his coming. He comes so as that he manifests himself, 'Behold'. And then he expects not that we should wake with that light and look out of ourselves, but he knocks, solicits us, at least with some noise at our doors, some calamities upon our neighbours. And again he appears not like a lightning that passes away as soon as it is seen, that no man can read by it nor work by it, nor light a candle, nor kindle a coal by it, but he stands at the door and expects us all day; not only with a patience but with a hunger to effect his purpose upon us. He would come in and sup with us, accept our diet, our poor endeavours; and then would have us sup with him, (as it is there added) would feast us with his abundant graces, which he brings even home to our doors. But those he does not give us at the door; not till we have let him in, by the good use of his former grace. And as he offers his fulness of his mercy by these means before, so by way of pardon and remission, if we have been defective in opening the door upon his standing and knocking, this fulness is fully expressed in this word of this text, as our two translations (neither departing from the natural signification of the word) have rendered it.

Punishment

This word is the same here, in David's sweetness, as in Cain's bitterness. And we cannot tell whether Cain speak there of a punishment too great to be borne, or of a sin too great to be pardoned; nor which David means here. It fills up the measure of God's mercy if we take him to mean both. God, upon confession, forgives the punishment of the sin; so that the just terror of hell and the imaginary terror of purgatory, for the next world, is taken away. And for this world, what calamities and tribulations soever fall upon us, after these confessions, and remissions, they have not the nature of punishments, but they are fatherly corrections and medicinal assistances against relapses, and have their main relation and prospect upon the future.

Iniquity

For not only the sin itself but the iniquity of the sin is said to be forgiven. God keeps nothing in his mind against the last day. But whatsoever is worst in the sin, the venom, the malignity of the sin, the violation of his law, the affrontings of his majesty residing in that law, though it have been a winking at his light, a resisting of his light, the ill nature, the malignity, the iniquity of the sin is forgiven. Only this remains, that God extinguishes not the right of a third person, or pardons a murder so as that he bars another from his appeal. Not that his pardon is not full, upon a full confession, but that the confession is no more full if it be not accompanied with satisfaction, that is restitution of all unjustly gotten, than if the confession lacked contrition and true sorrow. Otherwise the iniquity of the sin, and the punishment of the sin, are both fully pardoned. And so we have shut one leaf of this door, the fulness. The other is the speed and acceleration of his mercy, and that leaf we will clap to in a word.

Promptness

This is expressed in this, David is but at his speaking and God at his forgiving. David was but saying, nay but thinking, and God was doing, nay perfecting his work. To the lepers that cried out for mercy, Christ said 'Go, show yourselves to the priest'. So he put them into the way; and they went, says the text; and as they went they were healed upon the way. No man comes into the way but by illumination and direction of God. Christ put them into the way. The way is the Church. No man is cured out of the way; no man that separates himself from the Church; nor in the way neither, except he go. If he live negligently and trust only upon the outward profession; nor though he go, except he go according to Christ's bidding; except he conform himself to that worship of God, and to those means of sanctification, which God hath instituted in his Church, without singularities of his own or traditions of other men's inventing and imposing. This, this submitting and conforming ourselves to God, so as God hath commanded us, the purposing of this and the endeavouring of this, our saying that we will do it; and upon this purposing, this endeavouring, instantly, immediately, infallibly, follows God will, God does, God hath forgiven the iniquity and the punishment of the sin.

Therefore to end all, 'Pour out thy heart like water before the face of the Lord.' No liquor comes so clearly, so absolutely from the vessel, not oil, not milk, not wine, not honey, as that it leaves no taste behind; so may sweet sins. And therefore pour out, says the prophet, not the liquor, but the heart itself, and take a new heart of God's making. For thy former heart was never so of God's making as that Adam had not a hand in it. And his image was in it, in original sin as well as God's in creation. As liquors poured out leave a taste and a smell behind them, unperfected confessions (and who perfects his confession?) leave ill gotten goods sticking upon thine hair, and they leave a taste and a delight to think and speak of former sins, sticking upon thy self. But pour out thy heart like water; all ill impressions in the very root.

And for the accomplishment of this great mystery of godliness by confession, fix thy meditations upon those words, and in the strength of them come now (or when thou shalt be better strengthened by the meditation of them) to the table of the Lord. The Lord looketh upon men and if any say, 'I have sinned and perverted that which was right and it profited me not', he will deliver his soul from going down into the pit, and his life shall see light. And it is added, 'Lo all these things worketh God twice and thrice'. Here is a fulness of consolation, first plenary, and here is a present forgiveness. If man, if any man say, 'I have sinned', God doth, God forgives; and here is more than that, an iteration, if thou fall upon infirmity again God will on penitence more carefully performed forgive again. This he will do twice and thrice, says the Hebrew. Our translation might boldly say, as it doth, this God will do often. But yet if God find an over-confidence in this, God cannot be mocked, and therefore take heed of trusting upon it too often, but especially of trusting upon it too late. And whatsoever the Holy Ghost may mean by the twice or thrice, be sure to do it once, do it now, and receive thy Saviour there, and so as he offers himself unto thee in these ordinances this day, once, and twice, and thrice, that is in prayer, in preaching, in the sacrament. For this is thy trinity upon earth, that must bring thee to the Trinity in heaven.

DEATH'S DUEL

And unto God the Lord belong the issues of death.
Psalm 68:20

The Issue of Death

Buildings stand by the benefit of their foundations that sustain and support them, and of their buttresses that comprehend and embrace them, and of their contignations that knit and unite them. The foundations suffer them not to sink, the buttresses suffer them not to swerve, and the contignation and knitting suffers them not to cleave. The body of our building is in the former part of this verse. It is this: 'He that is our God is the God of salvation'; of salvations in the plural, so it is in the original: the God that gives us spiritual and temporal salvation too.

But of this building, the foundation, the buttresses, the contignations are in this part of the verse, which constitutes our text, and in the three divers acceptations of the words amongst our expositors. 'Unto God the Lord belong the issues of death.' For first the foundation of this building (that our God is the God of all salvations) is laid in this; that unto this 'God the Lord belong the issues of death', that is, it is in his power to give us an issue and deliverance, even then when we are brought to the jaws and teeth of death, and to the lips of that whirlpool, the grave. And so in this acceptation, this issue of death is a deliverance from death, and this is the most obvious and most ordinary acceptation of these words, and that upon which our translation lays hold, 'the issues from death'.

And then secondly the buttresses that comprehend and settle this building, that he that is our God, is the God of all salvation, are thus raised. 'Unto God the Lord belong the issues of death', that is, the disposition and manner of our death: what kind of issue and transmigration we shall have out of this world, whether prepared or sudden, whether violent or natural, whether in our perfect senses or shaken and disordered by sickness. There is no condemnation to be argued out of that, no judgement to be made upon that, for howsoever, they die, 'precious in his sight is the death of his saints', and with him are 'the issues of death', the ways of our departing out of this life are in his hands. And so in this sense of the words, this the issue of death is a deliverance in death. Not that God will deliver us from dying, but that he will have a care of us in the hour of death, of what kind soever our passage be.

And then lastly the contignation and knitting of this building, that he that is our God is the God of all salvations, consists in this, 'Unto this God the Lord belong the issues of death', that is, that this God the Lord having united and knit both natures in one, and being God, having also come into this world, in our flesh, he could have no other means to save us, he could have no other issue out of this world, nor return to his former glory, but by death. And so in this sense, this issue of death is a deliverance by death, by the death of this God, our Lord Christ Jesus. And this is St Augustine's acceptation of the words, and those many and great persons that have adhered to him.

In all these three lines then, we shall look upon these words. First, as the God of power, the Almighty Father rescues his servants from the jaws of death. And then as the God of mercy, the glorious Son rescued us, by taking upon himself this issue of death. And then between these two, as the God of comfort, the Holy Ghost rescues us from all discomfort by his blessed impressions beforehand, that what manner of death soever be ordained for us, yet this shall be an entrance into everlasting life. And these three considerations, our deliverance from death, in death, and by death, will abundantly do all the offices of the foundations, of the buttresses, of the contignation of this our building: that 'He that is our God is the God of all salvation' because 'unto this God the Lord belong the issues of death'.

From Death

First, then, we consider this issue of death to be deliverance from death, that with God the Lord are the issues of death, and therefore in all our deaths, and deadly calamities of this life, we may justly hope of a good issue from him. And all our periods and transitions in this life are so many passages from death to death. Our very birth and entrance into this life is an issue from death, for in our mother's womb we are dead so, as that we do not know we live, not so much as we do in our sleep. Neither is there any grave so close, or so putrid a prison, as the womb would be unto us if we stayed in it beyond our time, or died there before our time. In the grave the worms do not kill us, we breed and feed, and then kill those worms which we ourselves produced. In the womb the dead child kills the mother that conceived it. And if we be not dead so in the womb, so as that being dead we kill her that gave us our first life, our life of vegetation, yet we are dead so, as David's idols are dead. In the womb we are fitted for works of darkness, all the while deprived of light. And there in the womb we are taught cruelty, by being fed with blood, and may be damned, though we be never born.

Of our very making in the womb, David says, 'I am wonderfully and fearfully made', and 'Such knowledge is too excellent for me' for that 'is the Lord's doing, and it is wonderful in our eyes'. It is 'he that hath made us, and not we ourselves', no, nor our parents neither. 'Thy hands have made me and fashioned me round about' says Job, and (as the original word is) 'thou hast taken pains about me', and yet, says he, 'thou dost destroy me.' Though I be the masterpiece of the greatest Master (man is so), yet if you do no more for me, if you leave me where you made me, destruction will follow. The womb which should be the house of life becomes death itself if God leave us there. That which God threatens so often, the shutting of the womb, is not so heavy, nor so discomfortable a curse in the first, as in the latter shutting, nor in the shutting of barrenness, as in the shutting of weakness, when children are come to the birth and there is not strength to bring forth.

It is the exaltation of misery to fall from a near hope of happiness. And in that vehement imprecation, the prophet expresses the highest of God's anger, 'Give them O Lord, what wilt thou give them? give them a mis-carrying womb'. Therefore as soon as we are men (that is, inanimated, quickened in the womb), though we cannot ourselves, our parents have reason to say in our behalf, 'Wretched man that he is, who shall deliver him from this body of death?' for even the womb is a body of death if there be no deliverer. It must be he that said to Jeremiah, 'Before I formed thee I knew thee, and before thou camest out of the womb I sanctified thee'.

We are not sure that there was no kind of ship nor boat to fish in, nor to pass by, till God prescribed Noah that absolute form of the Ark. That word which the Holy Ghost, by Moses, uses for the Ark is common to all kinds of boats, and is the same word that Moses uses for the boat that he was exposed in, that his mother laid him in an ark of bulrushes. But we are sure that Eve had no midwife when she was delivered of Cain, therefore she might well say, 'I have gotten a man from the Lord', wholly, entirely from the Lord. It is the Lord that enabled me to conceive, the Lord that infused a quickening soul into that conception, the Lord that brought into the world that which himself had quickened. Without all this might Eve say, 'My body had been but the house of death', and to 'God the Lord belong the issues of death'.

But then this deliverance from that death, the death of the womb, is an entrance, a delivering over to another death, the manifold deaths of this world. We have a winding sheet in our mother's womb, which grows with us from our conception, and we come into the world, wound up in that winding sheet, for we come to seek a grave. And as prisoners discharged of actions may lie for fees, so when the womb has discharged us, yet we are bound to it by cords of flesh, by such a string, as that we cannot go thence, nor stay there. We celebrate our own funerals with cries, even at our birth; as though our three score and ten years life were spent in our mother's labour, and our circle made up in the first point thereof; we beg one baptism, with another, a sacrament of tears. And we come into a world that lasts many ages, but we last not.

'In my Father's house', says our blessed Saviour, speaking of heaven, . . . 'there are many mansions', divers and durable, so that if a man cannot possess a martyr's house (he has shed no blood for

Christ), yet he may have a confessor's, he has been ready to glorify God in the shedding of his blood. And if a woman cannot possess a virgin's house (she has embraced the holy state of marriage), yet she may have a matron's house, she has brought forth and brought up children in the fear of God.

'In my Father's house', in heaven, 'there are many mansions', but here upon earth, 'the son of man hath not where to lay his head', says he himself. How then has God given this earth to the sons of men? He has given them earth for their materials, to be made of earth, and he has given them earth for their grave and sepulchre, to return and resolve to earth, but not for their possession. 'Here we have no continuing city', nay no cottage that continues, nay no persons, no bodies that continue.

Even the Israel of God has no mansions, but journeys, pilgrimages in this life. By that measure did Jacob measure his life to Pharaoh: 'the days of the years of my pilgrimage'. And though the Apostle would not say that while we are in the body we are dead, yet he says while we are in the body, we are but in a pilgrimage, and we are absent from the Lord. He might have said dead, for this whole world is but an universal churchyard, but our common grave, and the life and motion that the greatest persons have in it is but as the shaking of buried bodies in the grave by an earthquake. That which we call life is but a week of deaths, seven days, seven periods of our life spent in dying, a dying seven times over; and there is an end. Our birth dies in infancy, and our infancy dies in youth, and youth and the rest die in age, and age also dies, and determines all.

Nor do all these, youth out of infancy, age out of youth, arise so, as a Phoenix out of the ashes of another Phoenix formerly dead, but as a wasp or a serpent out of a carrion, or as a snake out of dung. Our youth is worse than our infancy, and our age worse than our youth. Our youth is hungry and thirsty after those sins which our infancy knew not. And our age is sorry and angry that it cannot pursue those sins which our youth did. And besides all the way, so many deaths, that is, so many deadly calamities accompany every condition and every period of this life as that death itself would be an ease to them that suffer them. Upon this sense does Job wish that God had not given him an issue from the first death, from the womb. 'Wherefore hast thou brought me forth out of the womb? O that I had given up the ghost, and no eye seen me! I should have been as though I had not been.'

But if my case be as St Paul's case that 'I die daily', that something heavier than death falls upon me every day; if my case be David's case, 'all the day long we are killed', that not only every day, but every hour of the day something heavier than death falls upon me. though that be true of me, 'I was shapen in iniquity, and in sin did my mother conceive me', (there I died one death), though that be true of me, I was born not only of the child of sin, but the child of wrath, of the wrath of God for sin, which is a heavier death; yet with 'God the Lord are the issues of death', and after a Job, and a Joseph, and a Jeremiah, and a Daniel, I cannot doubt of a deliverance. And if no other deliverance conduce more to his glory and my good, yet he has the keys of death, and he can let me out at that door, that is, deliver me from the manifold deaths of this world, the every day's death and every hour's death, by that one death, the final dissolution of body and soul, the end of all.

But then is that the end of all? Is that dissolution of body and soul the last death that the body shall suffer? (For of spiritual death we speak not now.) It is not. Though it be an issue from the manifold deaths of this world, yet it is an entrance into the death of corruption and putrefaction and vermiculation and incineration, and dispersion in and from the grave, in which every dead man dies over again.

It was a prerogative peculiar to Christ not to die this death, not to see corruption. What gave him this privilege? Not Joseph's great proportion of gums and spices, that might have preserved his body from corruption and incineration longer than he needed it, longer than three days, but it would not have done it forever. What preserved him then? Did his exemption and freedom from original sin preserve him from this corruption and incineration? 'Tis true that original sin has induced this corruption and incineration upon us.

If we had not sinned in Adam, 'mortality had not put on immortality', (as the Apostle speaks), nor 'corruption had not put on incorruption', but we had had our transmigration from this to the other world, without any mortality and corruption at all.

But yet since Christ took sin upon him, so far as made him mortal, he had it so far too as might have made him see this corruption and incineration, though he had no original sin in himself. What preserved him then? Did the hypostatical union of both natures, God and man, preserve him from this corruption and incineration? 'Tis true that this was a most powerful embalming, to be embalmed with the divine nature itself, to be embalmed with eternity, was able to preserve him from corruption and incineration forever. And he was embalmed so, embalmed with the divine nature itself even in his body as well as in his soul; for the Godhead, the divine nature, did not depart, but remained still united to his dead body in the grave.

But yet for all this powerful embalming, this hypostatical union of both natures, we see Christ did die, and for all this union which made him God and man, he became no man (for the union of the body and soul makes the man, and he whose soul and body are separated by death as long as that state lasts is properly no man). And therefore, as in him the dissolution of body and soul was no dissolution of the hypostatical union, so is there nothing that constrains us to say, that though the flesh of Christ had seen corruption and incineration in the grave, this had been any dissolution of the hypostatical union, for the divine nature, the Godhead might have remained with all the elements and principles of Christ's body, as well as it did with the two constitutive parts of his person, his body and his soul.

This incorruption then was not in Joseph's gums and spices, nor was it in Christ's innocency and exemption from original sin, nor was it (that is, it is not necessary to say it was) in the hypostatical union. But this incorruptibleness of his flesh is most conveniently placed in 'thou wilt not suffer thy holy one to see corruption'. We look no further for causes or reasons in the mysteries of religion, but to the will and pleasure of God: Christ himself limited his inquisition in that, 'even so Father, for so it seemeth good in thy sight'. Christ's body did not see corruption, therefore, because God had decreed it should not.

The humble soul (and only the humble soul is the religious soul) rests himself upon God's purposes and his decrees which he has declared and manifested, not such as are conceived and imagined in ourselves, though upon some probability, some verisimilitude. So in our present case Peter proceeded in his sermon at Jerusalem, and so Paul in his at Antioch. They preached Christ to have been risen without seeing corruption not only because God had decreed it, but because he had manifested that decree in his prophet. Therefore does St Paul cite by special number the second Psalm for that decree. And therefore both St Peter and St Paul cite for it that place in the 16th Psalm, for when God declares his decree and purpose in the express words of his prophet, or when he declares it in the real execution of the decree, then he makes it ours, then he manifests it to us. And therefore as the mysteries of our religion are not the objects of our reason, but by faith we rest of God's decree and purpose (It is so, O God, because it is thy will it should be so), so God's decrees are ever to be considered in the manifestation thereof.

All manifestation is either in the word of God, or in the execution of the decree. And when these two concur and meet, it is the strongest demonstration that can be. When therefore I find those marks of adoption and spiritual filiation, which are delivered in the Word of God to be upon me, when I find that real execution of his good purpose upon me, as that actually I do live under the obedience, and under the conditions which are evidences of adoption and spiritual filiation; then, and so long as I see these marks and live so, I may safely comfort myself in a holy certitude and a modest infallibility of my adoption. Christ determines himself in that, the purpose of God was manifest to him. St Peter and St Paul determine themselves in those two ways of knowing the purpose of God, the Word of God before, the execution of the decree in the fulness of time. It was prophesied before, say they, and it is performed now. Christ is risen without seeing corruption.

Now this which is so singularly peculiar to him that his flesh should not see corruption, at his second coming, his coming to judgment, shall extend to all that are then alive, their flesh shall not see corruption, because as the Apostle says, and says as a secret, a mystery, 'Behold I show you a mystery, we shall not all sleep', (that is, not continue in the state of the dead in the grave), 'but we shall all be changed in an instant.' We shall have a dissolution, and in the same instant a redintegration, a recompacting of body and soul, and that shall be truly a death and truly a resurrection, but no sleeping, no corruption. But for us that die now and sleep in the state of the dead, we must all pass this posthumous death, this death after death, nay this death after burial, the dissolution after dissolution, this death of corruption and putrefaction, of vermiculation and incineration, of dissolution and dispersion in and from the grave, when these bodies that have been the children of royal parents, and the parents of royal children, must say with Job, 'Corruption thou art my father', and to the worm, 'Thou art my mother and my sister'

Miserable riddle, when the same worm must be my mother and my sister and myself. Miserable incest, when I must be married to my mother and my sister, and be both father and mother to my own mother and sister, beget and bear that worm which is all that miserable penury. When my mouth shall be filled with dust, and the worm shall feed, and feed sweetly upon me, when the ambitious man shall have no satisfaction if the poorest alive tread upon him, nor the poorest receive any contentment in being made equal to princes, for they shall be equal but in dust. One dies at his full strength, being wholly at ease and in quiet, and another dies in the bitterness of his soul, and never eats with pleasure, but they lie down alike in the dust and the worm covers them. In Job, and in Isaiah, it covers them and is spread under them, the worm is spread under you and the worm covers you. There's the mats and the carpets that lie under, and there's the state and the canopy that hangs over the greatest of the sons of men. Even those bodies that were the temples of the Holy Ghost come to this dilapidation, to ruin, to rubbish, to dust; even the Israel of the Lord, and Jacob himself has no other specification, no other denomination, but that 'worm of Jacob'.

Truly the consideration of this posthumous death, this death after burial, that after God (with whom are the issues of death) has delivered me from the death of the womb by bringing me into the world, and from the manifold deaths of the world by laying me in the grave, I must die again in an incineration of this flesh and in a dispersion of that dust. That that monarch who spread over many nations alive, must in his dust lie in a corner of that sheet of lead, and there but so long as that lead will last; and that private and retired man that thought himself his own forever, and never came forth, must in his dust of the grave be published and (such are the revolutions of the graves) be mingled with the dust of every highway, and of every dunghill, and swallowed in every puddle and pond: this is the most inglorious and contemptible vilification, the most deadly and peremptory nullification of man, that we can consider.

God seems to have carried the declaration of his power to a great height, when he sets the Prophet Ezekiel in the valley of dry bones and says, 'Son of man can these bones live?' as though it had been impossible, and yet they did. 'The Lord laid sinews upon them, and flesh, and breathed into them, and they did live.' But in that case there were bones to be seen, something visible, of which it might be said, Can this thing live? But in this death of incineration and dispersion of dust, we see nothing that we can call that man's. If we say, 'Can this dust live?' perchance it cannot. It may be the mere dust of the earth, which never did live, nor never shall. It may be the dust of that man's worms, which did live, but shall no more. It may be the dust of another man, that concerns not him of whom it is asked. This death of incineration and dispersion is, to natural reason, the most irrecoverable death of all, and yet 'unto God the Lord belong the issues of death', and by recompacting this dust into the same body, and reanimating the same body with the same soul, he shall in a blessed and glorious resurrection give me such an issue from this death as shall never pass into any other death, but establish me into a life that shall last as long as the Lord of life himself.

And so have you that that belongs to the first acceptation of these words ('unto God the Lord belong the issues of death'), that though from the womb to the grave and in the grave itself we pass from death to death, yet, as Daniel speaks, 'The Lord our God is able to deliver us, and he will deliver us.'

Delivered in Death

And so we pass unto our second accommodation of these words ('unto God the Lord belong the issues of death'), that it belongs to God and not to man, to pass a judgment upon us at our death, or to conclude a dereliction of God's part upon the manner thereof.

Those indications which the physicians receive, and those presagitions which they give for death or recovery in the patient, they receive and they give out of the grounds and the rules of their art. But we have no such rule or art to give a presagition of spiritual death and damnation upon any such indication as we see in any dying man. We see often enough to be sorry, but not to despair. For the mercies of God work momentarily in minutes, and many times insensibly to bystanders or any other than the party departing, and we may be deceived both ways. We used to comfort ourself in the death of a friend, if it be testified that he went away like a lamb, that is, without any reluctation. But, God knows that he may be accompanied with a dangerous damp and stupefaction, and insensibility of his present state. Our blessed Saviour suffered colluctations with death, and a sadness even in his soul to death, and an agony even to a bloody sweat in his body, and expostulations with God, and exclamations upon the cross.

He was a devout man, who said upon his death bed, or death turf (for he was a hermit) 'Hast thou served a good Master threescore and ten years, and now art thou loath to go into his presence?' Yet Hilarion was loath. He was a devout man, that said that day he died, . . . 'Consider this to be the first day's service that ever thou didst thy Master, to glorify him in a Christianly and a constant death, and if thy first day be thy last day too, how soon dost thou come to receive thy wages?' Yet Barlaam would have been content to have stayed longer for it.

Make no ill conclusions upon any man's loathness to die. And then, upon violent deaths inflicted, as upon malefactors, Christ himself has forbidden us by his own death to make any ill conclusion; for his own death had those impressions in it. He was reputed, he was executed as a malefactor, and no doubt many of them who concurred to his death did believe him to be so. Of sudden death there are scarce examples to be found in the Scriptures upon good men, for death in battle cannot be called sudden death. But God governs not by examples, but by rules, and therefore make no ill conclusion upon sudden death nor upon distempers neither, though perchance accompanied with some words of diffidence and distrust in the mercies of God.

The tree lies as it falls, 'tis true, but yet it is not the last stroke that fells the tree, nor the last word nor gasp that qualifies the soul. Still pray we for a peaceable life against violent death, and for time of repentance against sudden death, and for sober and modest assurance against distempered and diffident death, but never make ill conclusions upon persons overtaken with such deaths; 'to God the Lord belong the issues of death'. And he received Samson, who went out of this world in such a manner (consider it actively, consider it passively in his own death, and in those whom he slew with himself) as was subject to interpretation hard enough. Yet the Holy Ghost has moved St Paul to celebrate Samson in his great catalogue, and so does all the church.

Our critical day is not the very day of our death but the whole course of our life. I thank him that prays for me when my bell tolls, but I thank him much more that catechizes me, or preaches to me, or instructs me how to live. There's my security, the mouth of the Lord has said it, do this and you shall live. But though I do it, yet I shall die too, die a bodily, a natural death. But God never mentions, never seems to consider that death, the bodily, the natural death.

God does not say, live well and you shall die well, that is, an easy, a quiet death; but live well here, and you shall live well forever. As the first part of a sentence pieces well with the last, and never respects, never harkens after the parenthesis that comes between, so does a good life here flow into an eternal life, without any consideration what manner of death we die. But whether the gate of my prison be opened with an oiled key (by a gentle and preparing sickness), or the gate be hewn down by a violent death, or the gate be burned down by a raging and frantic fever, a gate into heaven I shall have, for from the Lord is the cause of my life, and with God the Lord are the issues of death. And further we carry not this second acceptation of the words, as this issue of death is a deliverance in death. God cares that the soul be safe, what agonies soever the body suffers in the hour of death.

Deliverance Through Death

But pass to our third part and last part: as this issue of death is a deliverance by the death of another, by the death of Christ. 'You have heard of the patience of Job', says St James. All this while you have done that, for in every man, calamitous, miserable man, a Job speaks. Now see 'the end of the Lord', says that Apostle, which is not that end that the Lord proposed to himself (salvation to us), nor the end which he proposes to us (conformity to him), but see 'the end of the Lord', says he, the end that the Lord himself came to; death and a painful and a shameful death.

But why did he die? and why die so? As St Augustine interpreting this text answers that question: because to this 'God our Lord belonged the issues of death'. What can be more obvious, more manifest than this sense of these words? In the former part of this verse, it is said, 'He that is our God, is the God of salvation', so he reads it, the God that must save us. Who can that be, says he, but Jesus? for therefore that name was given him, because he was to save us. And to this Jesus, says he, this Saviour, belong the issues of death. Being come into this life in our mortal nature, he could not go out of it any other way than by death. Therefore it is said, 'To

God the Lord belong the issues of death'; to show that his way to save us was to die. And from this text does St Isidor prove that Christ was truly man (which as many sects of heretics denied as that he was truly God), because to him, though he were (as the text doubles it) God the Lord, yet to him, to God the Lord belonged the issues of death. More cannot be said than Christ himself says of himself, 'These things Christ ought to suffer'; he had no other way but by death.

So then this part of our sermon must needs be a passion sermon. Since all his life was a continual passion, all our Lent may well be a continual Good Friday. Christ's painful life took off none of the pains of his death. He felt not the less then for having felt so much before. Nor will anything that shall be said before lessen, but rather enlarge the devotion to that which shall be said of his passion at the time of due solemnization thereof. Christ bled not a drop the less at the last for having bled at his circumcision before, nor will you shed a tear the less then, if you shed some now.

And therefore be now content to consider with me how to this God the Lord belonged the issues of death. That God, this Lord, the Lord of life could die, is a strange contemplation. That the Red Sea could be dry, that the sun could stand still, that an oven could be seven times heat and not burn, that lions could be hungry and not bite, is strange, miraculously strange, but super-miraculous that God could die. But that God would die is an exaltation of that. But even of that also it is a super-exaltation, that God should die, must die, and (said St Augustine), 'God the Lord had no issue but by death', and (says Christ himself), 'all this Christ ought to suffer', was bound to suffer. Says David, God is the God of revenges, he would not pass over the sin of man unrevenged, unpunished. But then (says that place) the God of revenges works freely, he punishes, he spares whom he will. And would he not spare himself? He would not. Love is strong as death, stronger; it drew in death that naturally is not welcome. 'If it be possible', says Christ, 'let this cup pass', when his love expressed in a former decree with his Father had made it impossible.

Many waters quench not love. Christ tried many. He was baptized out of his love, and his love determined not there. He mingled blood with water in his agony and that determined not his love. He wept pure blood, all his blood at all his eyes, at all his pores, in his flagellation and thorns (to the Lord our God belonged the issues of blood) and these expressed, but these did not quench his love. He would not spare, nay he could not spare himself. There was nothing more free, more voluntary, more spontaneous than the death of Christ. 'Tis true, he died voluntarily, but yet when we consider the contract that had passed between his Father and him, there was a kind of necessity upon him. All the Christ ought to suffer. And when shall we date this obligation, this necessity? When shall we say that began? Certainly this decree by which Christ was to suffer all this was an eternal decree, and was there anything before that, that was eternal? Infinite love, eternal love; be pleased to follow this home, and to consider it seriously, that what liberty soever we can conceive in Christ, to die or not to die, this necessity of dying, this decree is as eternal as that liberty; and yet how small a matter made he of this necessity and this dying?

His Father calls it but a bruise, and but a bruising of his heel ('the serpent shall bruise his heel') and yet that was that the serpent should practise and compass his death. Himself calls it but a baptism, as though he were to be the better for it. 'I have a baptism to be baptized with', and he was in pain till it was accomplished, and yet this baptism was his death. The Holy Ghost calls it joy ('for the joy which was set before him he endured the cross') which was not a joy of his reward after his passion, but a joy that filled him even in the midst of those torments, and arose from him. When Christ calls his passion a cup, and no worse ('can ye drink of my cup'), he speaks not odiously, not with detestation of it. Indeed it was a cup, a health to all the world. And, says David, 'what shall I render to the Lord?' Answer you with David, 'I will take a cup of salvation'. Take it, that cup of salvation, his passion, if not into your present imitation, yet into your present contemplation.

And behold how that Lord that was God yet could die, would

die, must die, for your salvation. That Moses and Elijah talked with Christ in the transfiguration both St Matthew and St Mark tell us but what they talked of only St Luke. Says he, 'They talked of his decease, of his death which was to be accomplished at Jerusalem.' Moses, who in his exodus had prefigured this issue of our Lord, and in passing Israel out of Egypt through the Red Sea had foretold in that actual prophecy Christ's passing of mankind through the sea of his blood. And Elijah, whose exodus and issue out of this world was a figure of Christ's ascension, had no doubt a great satisfaction in talking with our blessed Lord of the full consummation of all this in his death, which was to be accomplished at Jerusalem.

Our meditation of his death should be more visceral and affect us more because it is of a thing already done. The ancient Romans had a certain tenderness and detestation of the name of death, they could not name death, no, not in their wills. There they could not say 'if or when I die', but 'when the course of nature is accomplished upon me'. To us that speak daily of the death of Christ ('he was crucified, dead and buried'), can the memory or the mention of our own death be irksome or bitter? There are in these latter times amongst us those that name death freely enough, and the death of God, but in blasphemous oaths and execrations. Miserable men, who shall therefore be said never to have named Jesus, because they have named him too often, and therefore hear Jesus say, 'I never knew you', because they made themselves too familiar with him.

Moses and Elijah talked with Christ of his death only in a holy and joyful sense of the benefit which they and all the world were to receive by that. Discourses of religions should not be out of curiosity, but to edification. And then they talked with Christ of his death at that time, when he was in the greatest height of glory that ever he admitted in this world, that is, his transfiguration. And we are afraid to speak to the great men of this world of their death, but nourish in them a vain imagination of immortality and immutability. But (as St Peter said there) it is good to dwell here, in this consideration of his death, and therefore transfer we our tabernacle (our devotions) through some of those steps which God the Lord made to his issue of death that day.

Take in the whole day from the hour that Christ received the Passover upon Thursday, unto the hour in which he died the next day. Make this present day that day in your devotion, and consider what he did, and remember what you have done. Before he instituted and celebrated the Sacrament (which was after the eating of the Passover), he proceeded to that act of humility, to wash his disciples' feet, even Peter's, who for a while resisted him. In your preparation to the holy and blessed Sacrament, have you with a sincere humility sought a reconciliation with all the world, even with those that have been averse from it, and refused that reconciliation from you? If so, and not else, you have spent that first part of his last day in a conformity with him.

After the Sacrament he spent the time till night in prayer, in preaching, in psalms. Have you considered that a worthy receiving of the Sacrament consists in a continuation of holiness after, as well as in a preparation before? If so, you have therein also conformed yourself to him. So Christ spent his time till night: 'At night he went into the garden to pray', and he spent much time in prayer. How much? Because it is literally expressed that he prayed there three several times, and that returning to his disciples after his first prayer, and finding them asleep said, 'Could ye not watch with me one hour?', it is collected that he spent three hours in prayer. I dare scarce ask you where you went or how you disposed of yourself when it grew dark and after last night. If that time were spent in a holy recommendation of yourself to God and a submission of your will to his, it was spent in a conformity to him. In that time and in those prayers was his agony and bloody sweat. I will hope that you did pray, but not every ordinary and customary prayer; but prayer actually accompanied with shedding of tears, and dispositively in a readiness to shed blood for his glory in necessary case, puts you into a conformity with him.

About midnight he was taken and bound with a kiss. Are you not too comfortable to him in that? Is not that too literally, too exactly your case, at midnight to have been taken and bound with a kiss? From thence he was carried back to Jerusalem, first to Annas, then to Caiaphas, and (as late as it was) then he was examined and buffeted and delivered over to the custody of those officers, from whom he received all those irrisions and violences, the covering of his face, the spitting upon his face, the blasphemies of words, and the smartness of blows which that Gospel mentions. In which compass fell that crowing of the cock which called up Peter to his repentance. How you passed all that time last night, you know. If you did anything then that needed Peter's tears, and have not shed them, let me be your cock, do it now. Now your Master (in the unworthiest of his servants) looks back upon you, do it now.

Betimes, in the morning, so soon as it was day, the Jews held a counsel in the High Priest's hall, and agreed upon their evidence against him, and then carried him to Pilate, who was to be his judge. Did you accuse yourself when you waked this morning, and were you content even with false accusations (that is) rather to suspect actions to have been sin, which were not, than to smother and justify such as were truly sins? Then you spent that hour in conformity to him. Pilate found no evidence against him, and therefore to ease himself and to pass a compliment upon Herod, Tetrarch of Galilee, who was at that time at Jerusalem (because Christ being a Galilean was of Herod's jurisdiction) Pilate sent him to Herod, and rather as a madman than a malefactor. Herod remanded him (with scorns) to Pilate to proceed against him; and this was about eight of the clock.

Have you been content to come to this inquisition, this examination, this agitation, this pursuit of your conscience, to sift it, to follow it from the sins of your youth to your present sins, from the sins of your bed to the sins of your board, and from the substance to the circumstance of your sins? That's time spent like your Saviour's. Pilate would have saved Christ by using the privilege of the day in his behalf, because that day one prisoner was to be delivered, but they chose Barabbas. He would have saved him from death by satisfying their fury with inflicting other torments upon him, scourging and crowning with thorns, and loading him with many scornful and ignominious contumelies. But this redeemed him not, they pressed a crucifying.

Have you gone about to redeem your sin by fasting, by alms, by disciplines and mortifications, in way of satisfaction to the justice of God? That will not serve, that's not the right way; we press an utter crucifying of that sin that governs you, and that conforms you to Christ. Towards noon Pilate gave judgment, and they made such haste to execution, as that by noon he was upon the cross. There now hangs that sacred body upon the cross, rebaptized in his own tears and sweat, and embalmed in his own blood alive. There are those bowels of compassion, which are so conspicuous, so manifested, as that you may see them through his wounds. There those glorious eyes grew faint in their light; so as the sun, ashamed to survive them, departed with his light too. And then that Son of God, who was never from us, and yet had now come a new way unto us in assuming our nature, delivers that soul (which was never out of his Father's hands) by a new way, a voluntary emission of it into his Father's hands.

For though to this God our Lord, belonged these issues of death, so that considered in his own contract, he must necessarily die, yet at no breach or battery which they had made upon his sacred body issued his soul, but 'he gave up the Ghost', and as God breathed a soul into the first Adam, so this second Adam breathed his soul into God, into the hands of God. There we leave you in that blessed dependency, to hang upon him that hangs upon the cross, there bathe in his tears, there suck at his wounds, and lie down in peace in his grave, till he vouchsafe you a resurrection, and an ascension into the Kingdom, which he has purchased for you with the inestimable price of his incorruptible blood.

Devotions

1) THE FIRST ALTERATION, THE FIRST GRUDGING, OR THE SICKNESS

Meditation

Variable, and therefore miserable condition of man! this minute I was well, and am ill, this minute. I am surprised with a sudden change, and alteration to worse, and can impute it to no cause, nor call it by any name. We study health, and we deliberate upon our meats, and drink, and air and exercises, and we hew and we polish every stone that goes to that building; and so our health is a long and a regular work. But in a minute a cannon batters all, overthrows all, demolishes all. A sickness unprevented for all our diligence, unsuspected for all our curiosity, nay, undeserved, if we consider only disorder, summons us, seizes us, possesses us, destroys us in an instant. O miserable condition of man! which was not imprinted by God, who, as he is immortal himself, had put a coal, a beam of immortality into us, which we might have blown into a flame, but blew it out by our first sin. We beggared ourselves by hearkening after false riches, and infatuated ourselves by hearkening after false knowledge. So that now, we do not only die, but die upon the rack, die by the torment of sickness; nor that only, but are pre-afflicted, super-afflicted with these jealousies and suspicions and apprehensions of sickness, before we can call it a sickness. We are not sure we are ill; one hand asks the other by the pulse, and our eye asks our own urine how we do. O multiplied misery! We die, and cannot enjoy death, because we die in this torment of sickness. We are tormented with sickness, and cannot stay till the torment come, but pre-apprehensions and presages prophesy those torments which induce that death before either come; and our dissolution is conceived in these first changes, quickened in the sickness itself, and born in death, which bears date from these first changes. Is this the honour which man hath by being a little world, that he hath these earthquakes in himself, sudden shakings; these lightnings, sudden flashes; these thunders, sudden noises; these eclipses, sudden offuscations and darkening of his senses; these blazing stars, sudden fiery exhalations; these rivers of blood, sudden red waters? Is he a world to himself only therefore, that he hath enough in himself, not only to destroy and execute himself, but to presage that execution upon himself; to assist the sickness, to antedate the sickness, to make the sickness the more irremediable by sad apprehensions, and, as if he would make a fire the more vehement by sprinkling water upon the coals, so to wrap a hot fever in cold melancholy, lest the fever alone should not destroy fast enough without this contribution, nor perfect the work (which is destruction) except we joined an artificial sickness of our own melancholy, to our natural, our unnatural fever. O perplexed discomposition, O riddling distemper, O miserable condition of man!

Expostulation

If I were but mere dust and ashes I might speak unto the Lord, for the Lord's hand made me of this dust, and the Lord's hand shall recollect these ashes; the Lord's hand was the wheel upon which this vessel of clay was framed, and the Lord's hand is the urn in which these ashes shall be preserved. I am the dust and the ashes of the temple of the Holy Ghost, and what marble is so precious? But I am more than dust and ashes: I am my best part, I am my soul. And being so, the breath of God, I may breathe back these pious expostulations to my God: My God, my God, why is not my soul as sensible as my Body? Why hath not my soul these apprehensions, these presages, these changes, these antedates, these jealousies, these suspicions of a sin, as well as my body of a sickness? Why is there not always a pulse in my soul to beat at the approach of a temptation to sin? Why are there not always waters in mine eyes, to testify my spiritual sickness? I stand in the way of temptations, naturally, necessarily; all men do so; for there is a snake in every path, temptations in every vocation; but I go, I run, I fly into the ways of temptation which I might shun; nay, I break into houses where the plague is; I press into places of temptation, and tempt the devil himself, and solicit and importune them who had rather be left unsolicited by me. I fall sick of sin, and am bedded and bedrid, buried and putrified in the practice of sin, and all this while have no presage, no pulse, no sense of my sickness. O height, O depth of misery, where the first symptom of the sickness is hell, and where I never see the fever of lust, of envy, of ambition, by any other light than the darkness and horror of hell itself, and where the first messenger that speaks to me doth not say, 'Thou mayest die', no, nor 'Thou must die', but 'Thou art dead'; and where the first notice that my soul hath of her sickness is irrecoverableness, irremediableness: But, O my God, Job did not charge thee foolishly in his temporal afflictions, nor may I in my spiritual. Thou hast imprinted a pulse in our soul, but we do not examine it; a voice in our conscience, but we do not hearken unto it. We talk it out, we jest it out, we drink it out, we sleep it out; and when we wake, we do not say with Jacob, 'Surely the Lord is in this place, and I knew it not'; but though we might know it, we do not, we will not. But will God pretend to make a watch, and leave out the spring? to make so many various wheels in the faculties of the soul, and in the organs of the body, and leave out grace, that should move them? or will God make a spring, and not wind it up? Infuse his first grace, and not second it with more, without which we can no more use his first grace when we have it, than we could dispose ourselves by nature to have it? But alas, that is not our case; we are all prodigal sons, and not disinherited; we have received our portion, and misspent it, not been denied it. We are God's tenants here, and yet here, he our landlord, pays us rents; not yearly, nor quarterly, but hourly, and quarterly, every minute he renews his mercy, but we will not understand, lest that we should be converted, and he should heal us.

Prayer

O Eternal and most gracious God, who, considered in thyself, art a circle, first and last, and altogether; but, considered in thy working upon us, art a direct line, and leadest us from our beginning, through all our ways, to our end, enable me by thy grace to look forward to mine end, and to look backward too, to the considerations of thy mercies afforded me from the beginning; that so by that practice of considering thy mercy, in my beginning in this world, when thou plantedst me in the Christian church, and thy mercy in the beginning in the other world, when thou writest me in the book of life, in my election, I may come to a holy consideration of thy mercy in the beginning of all my actions here: that in all the beginnings, in all the accesses and approaches, of spiritual sicknesses of sin, I may hear and hearken to that voice, 'O thou man of God, there is death in the pot', and so refrain from that which I was so hungerly, so greedily flying to. 'A faithful ambassador is health', says thy wise servant Solomon. Thy voice received in the beginning of a sickness, of a sin, is true health. If I can see that light betimes, and hear that voice early, 'Then shall my light break forth as the morning, and my health shall spring forth speedily'. Deliver me therefore, O my God, from these vain imaginations; that it is an over-curious thing, a dangerous thing, to come to that tenderness, that rawness, that scrupulousness, to fear every concupiscence, every offer of sin, that this suspicious and jealous diligence will turn to an inordinate dejection of spirit, and a diffidence in thy care and providence; but keep me still established, both in a constant assurance, that thou wilt speak to me at the beginning of every such sickness, at the approach of every such sin; and that, if I take knowledge of that voice then, and fly to thee, thou wilt preserve me from falling, or raise me again, when by natural infirmity I am fallen. Do this, O Lord, for his sake, who knows our natural infirmities, for he had them, and knows the weight of our sins, for he paid a dear price for them, thy Son, our Saviour, Christ Jesus.

2) THE PHYSICIAN IS SENT FOR

Meditation

It is too little to call man a little world; except God, man is a diminutive to nothing. Man consists of more pieces, more parts, than the world; than the world doth, nay, than the world is. And if those pieces were extended, and stretched out in man as they are in the world, man would be the giant, and the world the dwarf; the world but the map, and the man the world. If all the veins in our bodies were extended to rivers, and all the sinews to veins of mines, and all the muscles that lie upon one another, to hills, and all the bones to quarries of stones, and all the other pieces to the proportion of those which correspond to them in the world, the air would be too little for this orb of man to move in, the firmament would be but enough for this star; for, as the whole world hath nothing, to which something in man doth not answer, so hath man many pieces of which the whole world hath no representation. Enlarge this meditation upon this great world, man, so far as to consider the immensity of the creatures this world produces; our creatures are our thoughts, creatures that are born giants; that reach from east to west, from earth to heaven; that do not only bestride all the sea and land, but span the sun and firmament at once; my thoughts reach all, comprehend all. Inexplicable mystery; I their creator am in a close prison, in a sick bed, any where, and any one of my creatures, my thoughts, is with the sun, and beyond the sun, overtakes the sun, and overgoes the sun in one pace, one step, everywhere. And then, as the other world produces serpents and vipers, malignant and venomous creatures, and worms and caterpillars, that endeavour to devour that world which produces them, and monsters compiled and complicated of divers parents and kinds; so this world, ourselves, produces all these in us, in producing diseases, and sicknesses of all those sorts: venomous and infectious diseases, feeding and consuming diseases, and manifold and entangled diseases, made up of many several ones. And can the other world name so many venomous, so many consuming, so many monstrous creatures, as we can diseases of all these kinds? O miserable abundance, O beggarly riches! how much do we lack of having remedies for every disease, when as yet we have not names for them? But we have a Hercules against these giants, these monsters; that is, the physician; he musters up all the forces of the other world to succour this, all nature to relieve man. We have the physician, but we are not the physician. Here we shrink in our proportion, sink in our dignity, in respect of very mean creatures, who are physicians to themselves. The hare that is pursued and wounded, they say, knows an herb, which being eaten throws off the arrow; a strange kind of vomit. The dog that pursues it, though he be subject to sickness, even proverbially, knows his grass that recovers him. And it may be true, that the drugger is as near to man as to other creatures; it may be that obvious and present simples, easy to be had, would cure him; but the apothecary is not so near him, nor the physician so near him, as they two are to other creatures. Man hath not that innate instinct, to apply those natural medicines to his present danger, as those inferior creatures have; he is not his own apothecary, his own physician, as they are. Call back therefore thy meditation again, and bring it down: what's become of man's great extent and proportion, when himself shrinks himself and consumes himself to a handful of dust; what's become of his soaring thoughts, his compassing thoughts, when himself brings himself to the ignorance, to the thoughtlessness, of the grave? His diseases are his own, but the physician is not; he hath them at home, but he must send for the physician.

Expostulation

I have not the righteousness of Job, but I have the desire of Job: 'I would speak to the Almighty, and I would reason with God.' My God, my God, how soon wouldst thou have me go to the physician, and how far wouldst thou have me go with the physician? I know thou hast made the matter, and the man, and the art; and I go not from thee when I go to the physician. Thou didst not make clothes before there was a shame of the nakedness of the body, but thou didst make physic before there was any grudging of any sickness; for thou didst imprint a medicinal virtue in many simples, even from the beginning. Didst thou mean that we should be sick when thou didst so? when thou madest them? No more than thou didst mean, that we should sin, when thou madest us: thou foresawest both, but causedst neither. Thou, Lord, promisest here trees, 'whose fruit shall be for meat, and their leaves for medicine'. It is the voice of thy Son, 'Wilt thou be made whole?' that draws from the patient a confession that he was ill, and could not make himself well. And it is thine own voice, 'Is there no physician?' that inclines us, disposes us, to accept thine ordinance. And it is the voice of the wise man, both for the matter, physic itself, 'The Lord hath created medicines out of the earth, and he that is wise shall not abhor them', and for the art, and the person, the physician cutteth off a long disease. In all these voices thou sendest us to those helps which thou hast afforded us in that. But wilt not thou avow that voice too, 'He that hath sinned against his Maker, let him fall into the hands of the physician', and wilt not thou afford me an understanding of those words? Thou, who sendest us for a blessing to the physician, dost not make it a curse to us to go when thou sendest. Is not the curse rather in this, that only he falls into the hands of the physician, that casts himself wholly, entirely upon the physician, confides in him, relies upon him, attends all from him, and neglects that spiritual physic which thou also hast instituted in thy Church. So to fall into the hands of the physician is a sin, and a punishment of former sins; so, as Asa fell, who in his disease 'sought not to the Lord, but to the physician'. Reveal therefore to me thy method, O Lord, and see whether I have followed it: that thou mayest have glory, if I have, and I pardon, if I have not, and help that I may. Thy method is, 'In time of thy sickness, be not negligent' wherein wilt thou have my diligence expressed? 'Pray unto the Lord, and he will make thee whole.' O Lord, I do; I pray, and pray thy servant David's prayer, 'Have mercy upon me O Lord, for I am weak; heal me, O Lord, for my bones are vexed': I know that even my weakness is a reason, a motive, to induce thy mercy, and my sickness an occasion of thy sending health. When art thou so ready, when is it so seasonable to thee, to commiserate, as in misery? But is prayer for health in season, as soon as I am sick? Thy method goes further: 'Leave off from sin, and order thy hands aright, and cleanse thy heart from all wickedness.' Have I, O Lord, done so? O Lord, I have; by thy grace, I am come to a holy detestation of my former sin. Is there any more? In thy method there is more: 'Give a sweet savour, and a memorial of fine flour, and make a fat offering, as not being.' And, Lord, by thy grace, I have done that, sacrificed a little of that little which thou lentest me, to them for whom thou lentest it; and now in thy method, and by thy steps, I am come to that, 'Then give place to the physician, for the Lord hath created him; let him not go from thee, for thou hast need of him.' I send for the physician, but I will hear him enter with those words of Peter, 'Jesus Christ maketh thee whole'; I long for his presence, but I look 'that the power of the Lord should be present to heal me'.

Prayer

O most mighty and most merciful God, who art so the God of health and strength, as that without thee all health is but the fuel, and all strength but the bellows of sin; behold me under the vehemence of two diseases, and under the necessity of two physicians, authorized by thee, the bodily, and the spiritual physician. I come to both as to thine ordinance, and bless and glorify thy name that, in both cases, thou hast afforded help to man by the ministry of man. Even in the new Jerusalem, in heaven itself, it hath pleased thee to discover a tree, which is 'a tree of life there, but the leaves thereof are for the healing of the nations'. Life itself is with thee there, for thou art life; and all kinds of health, wrought upon us here by thine instruments, descend from thence. 'Thou wouldst have healed Babylon, but she is not healed.' Take from me, O Lord, her perverseness, her wilfulness, her refractoriness, and hear thy Spirit saying in my soul: Heal me: O Lord, for I would be healed. 'Ephraim saw his sickness, and Judah his wound; then went Ephraim to the Assyrian, and sent to King Jareb, yet could not he heal you, nor cure you of your wound.' Keep me back, O Lord, from them who misprofess arts of healing the soul, or of the body, by means not imprinted by thee in the Church for the soul, or not in nature for the body. There is no spiritual health to be had by superstition, nor bodily by witchcraft; thou, Lord, and only thou, art Lord of both. Thou in thyself art Lord of both, and thou in thy Son art the physician, the applier of both. 'With his stripes we are healed', says the prophet there; there, before he was scourged, we were healed with his stripes; how much more shall I be healed now, now when that which he hath already suffered actually is actually and effectually applied to me? Is there any thing incurable, upon which that balm drops? Any vein so empty as that that blood cannot fill it? Thou promisest to heal the earth; but it is when the inhabitants of the earth 'pray that thou wouldst heal it'. Thou promisest to heal their waters, but 'their miry places and standing waters', thou sayest there, 'thou wilt not heal'. My returning to any sin, if I should return to the ability of sinning over all my sins again thou wouldst not pardon. Heal this earth, O my God, by repentant tears, and heal these waters, these tears, from all bitterness, from all diffidence, from all dejection, by establishing my irremovable assurance in thee. 'Thy Son went about healing all manner of sickness.' (No disease incurable, none difficult; he healed them in passing.) 'Virtue went out of him, and he healed all', all the multitude (no person incurable), he healed them 'every whit' (as himself speaks), he left no relics of the disease; and will this universal physician pass by this hospital, and not visit me? not heal me? not heal me wholly? Lord, I look not that thou shouldst say by thy messenger to me, as to Hezekiah, 'Behold, I will heal thee, and on the third day thou shalt go up to the house of the Lord.' I look not that thou shouldst say to me, as to Moses in Miriam's behalf, when Moses would have had her healed presently, 'If her father had but spit in her face, should she not have been ashamed seven days? Let her be shut up seven days, and then return', but if thou be pleased to multiply seven days (and seven is infinite), if this day must remove me till days shall be no more, seal to me my spiritual health, in affording me the seals of thy Church; and for my temporal health, prosper thine ordinance, in their hands who shall assist in the sickness, in that manner, and in that measure, as may most glorify thee, and most edify those who observe the issues of thy servants, to their own spiritual benefit.

3) UPON THE PHYSICIANS' CONSULTATION THEY PRESCRIBE

Meditation

They have seen me and heard me, arraigned me in these fetters and received the evidence; I have cut up mine own anatomy, dissected myself, and they are gone to read upon me. O how manifold and perplexed a thing, nay, how wanton and various a thing, is ruin and destruction! God presented to David three kinds, war, famine and pestilence; Satan left out these, and brought in fires from heaven and winds from the wilderness. If there were no ruin but sickness, we see the masters of that art can scarce number, not name all sicknesses; every thing that disorders a faculty, and the function of that, is a sickness; the names will not serve them which are given from the place affected, the pleurisy is so; nor from the effect which it works, the falling sickness is so; they cannot have names enough, from what it does, nor where it is, but they must extort names from what it is like, what it resembles, and but in some one thing, or else they would lack names; for the wolf, and the canker, and the polypus are so; and that question whether there be more names or things, is as perplexed in sicknesses as in any thing else, except it be easily resolved upon that side that there are more sicknesses than names. If ruin were reduced to that one way, that man could perish no way but by sickness, yet his danger were infinite; and if sickness were reduced to that one way, that there were no sickness but a fever, yet the way were infinite still; for it would overload and oppress any natural disorder and discompose any artificial memory, to deliver the names of several fevers; how intricate a work then have they who are gone to consult which of these sicknesses mine is; and then which of these fevers, and then what it would do, and then how it may be countermined. But even in ill it is a degree of good when the evil will admit consultation. In many diseases, that which is but an accident, but a symptom of the main disease, is so violent, that the physician must attend the cure of that, though he pretermit (so far as to intermit) the cure of the disease itself. Is it not so in states too? Sometimes the insolency of those that are great puts the people into commotions; the great disease, and the greatest danger to the head, is the insolency of the great ones; and yet they execute martial law, they come to present executions upon the people, whose commotion was indeed but a symptom, but an accident of the main disease; but this symptom, grown so violent, would allow no time for a consultation. Is it not so in the accidents of the diseases of our mind too? Is it not evidently so in our affections, in our passions? If a choleric man be ready to strike, must I go about to purge his choler, or to break the blow? But where there is room for consultation things are not desperate. They consult, so there is nothing rashly, inconsiderately done; and then they prescribe, they write, so there is nothing covertly, disguisedly, unavowedly done. In bodily diseases it is not always so; sometimes, as soon as the physician's foot is in the chamber, his knife is in the patient's arm; the disease would not allow a minute's forbearing of blood, nor prescribing of other remedies. In states and matter of government it is so too, they are sometimes surprised with such accidents, as that the magistrate asks not what may be done by law, but does that which must necessarily be done in that case. But it is a degree of good in evil, a degree that carries hope and comfort in it, when we may have recourse to that which is written, and that the proceedings may be apt, and ingenuous, and candid, and avowable, for that gives satisfaction and acquiescence. They who have received my anatomy of myself consult, and end their consultation in prescribing, and in prescribing physic; proper and convenient remedy; for if they should come in again and chide me for some disorder that had occasioned and induced, or that had hastened and exalted this sickness, or if they should begin to write new rules for my diet and exercise when I were well, this were to antedate or to postdate their consultation, not to give physic. It were rather a vexation than a relief, to tell a condemned prisoner, You might have lived if you had done this; and if you can get your pardon, you shall do well to take this or this course hereafter. I am glad they know (I have hid nothing from them), glad they consult (they hide nothing from one another), glad they write (they hide nothing from the world), glad that they write and prescribe physic, that there are remedies for the present case.

Expostulation

My God, my God, allow me a just indignation, a holy detestation of the insolency of that man who, because he was of that high rank, of whom thou hast said, 'They are gods', thought himself more than equal to thee; that king of Aragon, Alphonsus, so perfect in the motions of the heavenly bodies as that he adventured to say, that if he had been of counsel with thee, in the making of the heavens, the heavens should have been disposed in a better order than they are. The King Hezekiah would not endure thy prophet to reprehend him, but asked him in anger, 'Art thou made of the king's counsel?' When thy prophet Isaiah asks that question, 'Who hath directed the spirit of the Lord, or being his counsellor hath taught him?' it is after he had settled and determined that office upon thy Son, and him only, when he joins with those great titles, the mighty God and the Prince of peace, this also, the Counsellor; and after he had settled upon him the spirit of might and of counsel. So that then thou, O God, though thou have no counsel from man, yet dost nothing upon man without counsel. In the making of man there was a consultation; 'Let us make man.' In the preserving of man, 'O thou great Preserver of men', thou proceedest by counsel; for all thy external works are the works of the whole Trinity, and their hand is to every action. How much more must I apprehend that all you blessed and glorious persons of the Trinity are in consultation now, what you will do with this infirm body, with this leprous soul, that attends guiltily, but yet comfortably, your determination upon it. I offer not to counsel them who meet in consultation for my body now, but I open my infirmities, I anatomize my body to them. So I do my soul to thee, O my God, in an humble confession, that there is no vein in me that is not full of the blood of thy Son, whom I have crucified and crucified again, by multiplying many, and often repeating the same, sins; that there is no artery in me that hath not the spirit of error, the spirit of lust, the spirit of giddiness in it, no bone in me that is not hardened with the custom of sin and nourished and supplied with the marrow of sin; no sinews, no ligaments, that do not tie and chain sin and sin together. Yet, O blessed and glorious Trinity, O holy and whole college, and yet but one physician, if you take this confession into a consultation, my case is not desperate, my destruction is not decreed. If your consultation determine in writing, if you refer me to that which is written, you intend my recovery: for all the way, O my God (ever constant to thine own ways), thou hast proceeded openly, intelligibly, manifestly by the book. From thy first book, the book of life, never shut to thee, but never thoroughly open to us; from thy second book, the book of nature, where, though sub-obscurely and in shadows, thou hast expressed thine own image; from thy third book, the Scriptures, where thou hadst written all in the Old, and then lightedst us a candle to read it by, in the New, Testament; to these thou hadst added the book of just and useful laws, established by them to whom thou hast committed thy people; to those, the manuals, the pocket, the bosom books of our own consciences; to those thy particular books of all our particular sins; and to those, the books with seven seals, which only 'the Lamb which was slain, was found worthy to open'; which, I hope, it shall not disagree with the meaning of thy blessed Spirit to interpret the promulgation of their pardon and righteousness who are washed in the blood of that Lamb; and if thou refer me to these books, to a new reading, a new trial by these books, this fever may be but a burning in the hand and I may be saved, though not by my book, mine own conscience, nor by thy other books, yet by thy first, the book of life, thy decree for my election, and by thy last, the book of the Lamb, and the shedding of his blood upon me. If I be still under consultation, I am not condemned yet; if I be sent to these books, I shall not be condemned at all; for though there be something written in some of those books (particularly in the Scriptures) which some men turn to poison, yet upon these consultations (these confessions, these takings of our particular cases into thy consideration) thou intendest all for physic; and even from those sentences from which a too late repenter will suck desperation, he that seeks thee early shall receive thy morning dew, thy seasonable mercy, thy forward consolation.

Prayer

O Eternal and most gracious God, who art of so pure eyes as that thou canst not look upon sin, and we of so unpure constitutions as that we can present no object but sin, and therefore might justly fear that thou wouldst turn thine eyes for ever from us, as, though we cannot endure afflictions in ourselves, yet in thee we can; so, though thou canst not endure sin in us, yet in thy Son thou canst, and he hath taken upon himself, and presented to thee, all those sins which might displease thee in us. There is an eye in nature that kills as soon as it sees, the eye of a serpent; no eye in nature that nourishes us by looking upon us; but thine eye, O Lord, does so. Look therefore upon me, O Lord, in this distress and that will recall me from the borders of this bodily death; look upon me, and that will raise me again from that spiritual death in which my parents buried me when they begot me in sin, and in which I have pierced even to the jaws of hell by multiplying such heaps of actual sins upon that foundation, that root of original sin. Yet take me again into your consultation, O blessed and glorious Trinity; and though the Father know that I have defaced his image received in my creation; though the Son know I have neglected mine interest in the redemption; yet, O blessed Spirit, as thou art to my conscience so be to them, a witness that, at this minute, I accept that which I have so often, so rebelliously refused, thy blessed inspirations; be thou my witness to them that, at more pores than this slack body sweats tears, this sad soul weeps blood; and more for the displeasure of my God, than for the stripes of his displeasure. Take me, then, O blessed and glorious Trinity, into a reconsultation, and prescribe me any physic. If it be a long and painful holding of this soul in sickness, it is physic if I may discern thy hand to give it; and it is physic if it be a speedy departing of this soul, if I may discern thy hand to receive it.

4) FROM THE BELLS OF THE CHURCH ADJOINING, I AM DAILY REMEMBERED OF MY BURIAL IN THE FUNERALS OF OTHERS

Meditation

We have a convenient author, who writ a discourse of bells when he was prisoner in Turkey. How would he have enlarged himself if he had been my fellow-prisoner in this sick bed, so near to that steeple which never ceases, no more than the harmony of the spheres, but is more heard. When the Turks took Constantinople, they melted the bells into ordnance; I have heard both bells and ordnance, but never been so much affected with those as with these bells. I have lain near a steeple in which there are said to be more than thirty bells, and near another, where there is one so big, as that the clapper is said to weigh more than six hundred pounds, yet never so affected as here. Here the bells can scarce solemnize the funeral of any person, but that I knew him, or knew that he was my neighbour; we dwelt in houses near to one another before, but now he is gone into that house into which I must follow him. There is a way of correcting the children of great persons, that other children are corrected in their behalf, and in their names, and this works upon them who indeed had more deserved it. And when these bells tell me, that now one, and now another is buried, must not I acknowledge that they have the correction due to me, and paid the debt that I owe? There is a story of a bell in a monastery which, when any of the house was sick to death, rung always voluntarily, and they knew the inevitableness of the danger by that. It rung once when no man was sick, but the next day one of the house fell from the steeple and died, and the bell held the reputation of a prophet still. If these bells that warn to a funeral now, were appropriated to none, may not I, by the hour of the funeral, supply? How many men that stand at an execution, if they would ask, For what dies that man? should hear their own faults condemned, and see themselves executed by attorney? We scarce hear of any man preferred, but we think of ourselves that we might very well have been that man; why might not

I have been that man that is carried to his grave now? Could I fit myself to stand or sit in any man's place, and not to lie in any man's grave? I may lack much of the good parts of the meanest, but I lack nothing of the mortality of the weakest; they may have acquired better abilities than I, but I was born to as many infirmities as they. To be an incumbent by lying down in a grave, to be a doctor by teaching mortification by example, by dying, though I may have seniors, others may be older than I, yet I have proceeded apace in a good university, and gone a great way in a little time, by the furtherance of a vehement fever, and whosoever these bells bring to the ground today, if he and I had been compared yesterday, perchance I should have been thought likelier to come to this preferment then than he. God hath kept the power of death in his own hands, lest any man should bribe death. If man knew the gain of death, the ease of death, he would solicit, he would provoke death to assist him by any hand which he might use. But as when men see many of their own professions preferred, it ministers a hope that that may light upon them; so when these hourly bells tell me of so many funerals of men like me, it presents, if not a desire that it may, yet a comfort whensoever mine shall come.

Expostulation

My God, my God, I do not expostulate with thee, but with them who dare do that; who dare expostulate with thee, when in the voice of thy Church thou givest allowance to this ceremony of bells at funerals. Is it enough to refuse it, because it was in use among the Gentiles? so were funerals too. Is it because some abuses may have crept in amongst Christians? Is that enough, that their ringing hath been said to drive away evil spirits? Truly, that is so far true, as that the evil spirit is vehemently vexed in their ringing, therefore, because that action brings the congregation together, and unites God and his people, to the destruction of that kingdom which the evil spirit usurps. In the first institution of thy Church in this world, in the foundation of thy militant Church amongst the Jews, thou didst appoint the calling of the assembly in to be by trumpet;

and when they were in, then thou gavest them the sound of bells in the garment of thy priest. In the triumphant Church, thou employest both too, but in an inverted order; we enter into the triumphant Church by the sound of bells (for we enter when we die); and then we receive our further edification, or consummation, by the sound of trumpets at the resurrection. The sound of thy trumpets thou didst impart to secular and civil uses too, but the sound of bells only to sacred. Lord, let not us break the communion of saints in that which was intended for the advancement of it; let not that pull us asunder from one another, which was intended for the assembling of us in the militant, and associating of us to the triumphant Church. But he, for whose funeral these bells ring now, was at home, at his journey's end yesterday; why ring they now? a man, that is a world, is all the things in the world; he is an army, and when an army marches, the van may lodge tonight where the rear comes not till tomorrow. A man extends to his act and to his example; to that which he does, and that which he teaches; so do those things that concern him, so do these bells; that which rung yesterday was to convey him out of the world in his van, in his soul; that which rung today was to bring him in his rear, in his body, to the church; and this continuing of ringing after his entering is to bring him to me in the application. Where I lie I could hear the psalm, and did join with the congregation in it; but I could not hear the sermon, and these latter bells are a repetition sermon to me. But, O my God, my God, do I that have this fever need other remembrances of my mortality? Is not mine own hollow voice, voice enough to pronounce that to me? Need I look upon a death's head in a ring, that have one in my face? or go for death to my neighbour's house, that have him in my bosom? We cannot, we cannot, O my God, take in too many helps for religious duties; I know I cannot have any better image of thee than thy Son, nor any better image of him than his Gospel; yet must not I with thanks confess to thee, that some historical pictures of his have sometimes put me upon better meditations than otherwise I should have fallen upon? I know thy Church needed not to have taken in, from Jew, or

Gentile, any supplies for the exaltation of thy glory, or our devotion; of absolute necessity I know she needed not; but yet we owe thee our thanks, that thou hast given her leave to do so, and that as, in making us Christians, thou didst not destroy that which we were before, natural men, so, in the exalting of our religious devotions now we are Christians, thou hast been pleased to continue to us those assistances which did work upon the affections of natural men before; for thou lovest a good man as thou lovest a good Christian; and though grace be merely from me, yet thou dost not plant grace but in good natures.

Prayer

O eternal and most gracious God, who having consecrated our living bodies to thine own Spirit, and made us temples of the Holy Ghost, dost also require a respect to be given to these temples, even when the priest is gone out of them, to these bodies when the soul is departed from them, I bless and glorify thy name, that as thou takest care in our life of every hair of our head, so dost thou also of every grain of ashes after our death. Neither dost thou only do good to us all in life and death, but also wouldst have us do good to one another, as in a holy life, so in those things which accompany our death. In that contemplation I make account that I hear this dead brother of ours, who is now carried out to his burial, to speak to me, and to preach my funeral sermon in the voice of these bells. In him, O God, thou hast accomplished to me even the request of Dives to Abraham; thou hast sent one from the dead to speak unto me. He speaks to me aloud from the steeple; he whispers to me at these curtains, and he speaks thy words: 'Blessed are the dead which die in the Lord from henceforth.' Let this prayer, therefore, O my God, be as my last gasp, my expiring, my dying in thee; that if this be the hour of my transmigration, I may die the death of a sinner, drowned in my sins, in the blood of thy Son; and if I live longer, yet I may now die the death of the righteous, die to sin; which death is a resurrection to a new life. 'Thou killest and thou givest life': which soever comes, it comes from thee, which way soever it comes, let me come to thee.

5) NOW, THIS BELL TOLLING SOFTLY FOR ANOTHER, SAYS TO ME: THOU MUST DIE

Meditation

Perchance he for whom this bell tolls may be so ill, as that he knows not it tolls for him; and perchance I may think myself so much better than I am, as that they who are about me, and see my state, may have caused it to toll for me, and I know not that. The Church is Catholic, universal, so are all her actions; all that she does belongs to all. When she baptizes a child, that action concerns me, for that child is thereby connected to that body which is my head too, and ingrafted into that body whereof I am a member. And when she buries a man, that action concerns me; all mankind is of one author, and is one volume; when one man dies, one chapter is not torn out of the book, but translated into a better language; and every chapter must be so translated. God employs several translators; some pieces are translated by age, some by sickness, some by war, some by justice; but God's hand is in every translation, and his hand shall bind up all our scattered leaves again for that library where every book shall lie open to one another. As therefore the bell that rings to a sermon calls not upon the preacher only, but upon the congregation to come, so this bell calls us all; but how much more me, who am brought so near the door by this sickness. There was a contention as far as a suit (in which both piety and dignity, religion and estimation, were mingled), which of the religious orders should ring to prayers first in the morning; and it was determined, that they should ring first that rose earliest. If we understand aright the dignity of this bell that tolls for our evening prayer, we would be glad to make it ours by rising early, in that application, that it might be ours as well as his, whose indeed it is. The bell doth toll for him that thinks it doth; and though it intermit again, yet from that minute that that occasion wrought upon him, he is united to God. Who casts not up his eye to the sun when it rises? but who takes off his eye from a comet when that breaks out? Who bends not his ear to any bell which upon any occasion rings? but who can remove it from that bell which is passing a piece of himself out of this world? No man is an island, entire of itself; every man is a piece of the continent, a part of the main. If a clod be washed away by the sea, Europe is the less, as well as if a promontory were, as well as if a manor of thy friend's or of thine own were: any man's death diminishes me, because I am involved in mankind, and therefore never send to know for whom the bell tolls; it tolls for thee. Neither can we call this a begging of misery, or a borrowing of misery, as though we were not miserable enough of ourselves, but must fetch in more from the next house, in taking upon us the misery of our neighbours. Truly it were an excusable covetousness if we did, for affliction is a treasure, and scarce any man hath enough of it. No man hath affliction enough that is not matured and ripened by it, and made fit for God by that affliction. If a man carry treasure in bullion, or in a wedge of gold, and have none coined into current money, his treasure will not defray him as he travels. Tribulation is treasure in the nature of it, but it is not current money in the use of it, except we get nearer and nearer our home, heaven, by it. Another man may be sick too, and sick to death, and this affliction may lie in his bowels, as gold in a mine, and be of no use to him; but this bell, that tells me of his affliction, digs out and applies that gold to me; if by this consideration of another's danger I take mine own into contemplation, and so secure myself, by making my recourse to my God, who is our only security.

Expostulation

My God, my God, is this one of thy ways of drawing light out of darkness, to make him for whom this bell tolls, now in this dimness of his sight, to become a superintendent, an overseer, a bishop, to as many as hear his voice in this bell, and to give us a confirmation in this action? Is this one of thy ways, to raise strength out of weakness, to make him who cannot rise from his bed, nor stir in his bed, come home to me, and in this sound give me the strength of healthy and vigorous instructions? O my God, my God, what thunder is not a well-tuned cymbal, what hoarseness, what harshness, is not a clear organ, if thou be pleased to set thy voice to it? And what organ is not well played on if thy hand be upon it? Thy voice, thy hand, is in this sound, and in this one sound I hear this whole concert. I hear thy Jacob call unto his sons and say, 'Gather yourselves together, that I may tell you what shall befall you in the last days': he says, That which I am now, you must be then. I hear thy Moses telling me, and all within the compass of this sound, 'This is the blessing wherewith I bless you before my death'; this, that before your death, you would consider your own in mine. I hear thy prophet saying to Hezekiah, 'Set thy house in order, for thou shalt die, and not live': he makes use of his family, and calls this a setting of his house in order, to compose us to the meditation of death. I hear thy apostle saying, 'I think it meet to put you in remembrance, knowing that shortly I must go out of this tabernacle': this is the publishing of his will, and this bell is our legacy, the applying of his present condition to our use. I hear that which makes all sounds music, and all music perfect; I hear thy Son himself saying, 'Let not your hearts be troubled'; only I hear this change, that whereas thy Son says there, 'I go to prepare a place for you', this man in this sound says, I send to prepare you for a place, for a grave. But, O my God, my God, since heaven is glory and joy, why do not glorious and joyful things lead us, induce us to heaven? Thy legacies in thy first will, in the Old Testament, were plenty and victory, wine and oil, milk and honey, alliances of friends, ruin of enemies, peaceful hearts and cheerful countenances, and by these galleries thou broughtest them into thy bedchamber, by these glories and joys, to the joys and glories of heaven. Why hast thou changed thine old ways, and carried us by the ways of discipline and mortification, by the ways of mourning and lamentation, by the ways of miserable ends and miserable anticipations of those miseries, in appropriating the exemplar miseries of others to ourselves, and usurping upon their miseries as our own, to our prejudice? Is the glory of heaven no perfecter in itself, but that it needs a foil of depression and ingloriousness in this world, to set it off? Is the joy of heaven no perfecter in itself, but that it needs the sourness of this life to give it a taste? Is that joy and that glory but a comparative glory and a comparative joy? not such in itself, but such in comparison of the joylessness and the ingloriousness of this world? I know, my God, it is far, far otherwise. As thou thyself, who art all, art made of no substances, so the joys and glory which are with thee are made of none of these circumstances, essential joy, and glory essential. But why then, my God, wilt thou not begin them here? Pardon, O God, this unthankful rashness; I that ask why thou dost not, find even now in myself, that thou dost; such joy, such glory, as that I conclude upon myself, upon all, they that find not joys in their sorrows, glory in their dejections in this world, are in a fearful danger of missing both in the next.

Prayer

O eternal and most gracious God, who hast been pleased to speak to us, not only in the voice of nature, who speaks in our hearts, and of thy word, which speaks to our ears, but in the speech of speechless creatures, in Balaam's ass, in the speech of unbelieving men, in the confession of Pilate, in the speech of the devil himself, in the recognition and attestation of thy Son, I humbly accept thy voice in the sound of this sad and funeral bell. And first, I bless thy glorious name, that in this sound and voice I can hear thy instructions, in another man's to consider mine own condition; and to know, that this bell which tolls for another, before it come to ring out, may take me in too. As death is the wages of sin it is due to me; as death is the end of sickness it belongs to me; and though so disobedient a servant as I may be afraid to die, yet to so merciful a master as thou I cannot be afraid to come; and therefore into thy hands, O my God, I commend my spirit, a surrender which I know thou wilt accept, whether I live or die, for thy servant David made it, when he put himself into thy protection for his life; and thy blessed Son made it, when he delivered up his soul at his death: declare thou thy will upon me, O Lord, for life or death in thy time: receive my surrender of myself now; into thy hands, O Lord I commend my spirit. And being thus, O my God, prepared by thy correction, mellowed by thy chastisement, and conformed to thy will by thy Spirit, having received thy pardon for my soul, and asking no reprieve for my body, I am bold, O Lord, to bend my prayers to thee for his assistance, the voice of whose bell hath called me to his devotion. Lay hold upon his soul, O God, till that soul have thoroughly considered his account; and how few minutes soever it have to remain in that body, let the power of thy Spirit recompense the shortness of time, and perfect his account before he pass away; present his sins so to him, as that he may know what thou forgivest, and not doubt of thy forgiveness, let him stop upon the infiniteness of those sins, but dwell upon the infiniteness of thy mercy; let him discern his own demerits, but wrap himself up in the merits of thy Son Christ Jesus; breathe inward comforts to his heart, and afford him the power of giving such outward testimonies thereof, as all that are about him may derive comforts from thence, and have this edification, even in this dissolution, that though the body be going the way of all flesh, yet that soul is going the way of all saints. When thy Son cried out upon the cross, 'My God, my God, why hast thou forsaken me?' he spake not so much in his own person, as in the person of the Church, and of his afflicted members, who in deep distresses might fear thy forsaking. This patient, O most blessed God, is one of them; in his behalf, and in his name, hear thy Son crying to thee, 'My God, my God, why hast thou forsaken me?' and forsake him not; but with thy left hand lay his body in the grave (if that be thy determination upon him), and with thy right hand receive his soul into the kingdom, and unite him and us in one communion of saints. Amen.